FIVE
MINUTE
CHALLENGE
#1

FIVE
MINUTE
CHALLENGE
#1

KEN WEBER

Stoddart

Published in 1997 by Stoddart Publishing Co. Limited
34 Lesmill Road, Toronto, Canada M3B 2T6

Distributed in Canada by General Distribution Services Limited
34 Lesmill Road, Toronto, Canada M3B 2T6
Tel. (416) 445-3333 Fax (416) 445-5967
E-mail Customer.Service@ccmailgw.genpub.com

Distributed in the U.S. by General Distribution Services Inc.
85 River Rock Drive, Suite 202, Buffalo, New York 14207
Toll-free tel. 1-800-805-1083 Toll-free fax 1-800-481-6207
E-mail gdsinc@genpub.com

01 00 99 98 97 1 2 3 4 5

Cataloging in Publication Data

Weber, K. J. (Kenneth Jerome), 1940–
Five-minute challenge #1

ISBN 0-7737-5907-7

1. Questions and answers. I. Title.

GV1507.Q5W42 1997   031.02   97-931966-8

Cover design: Bill Douglas @ The Bang
Text design: Tannice Goddard

Printed and bound in Canada

*We gratefuly acknowledge the Canada Council for the Arts and the
Ontario Arts Council for their support of our publishing program.*

To the poker-playing pals
of Palgrave . . .
If only nations got along as well . . .

◁ Introduction ▷

For sure, you know it was Jackie Robinson who broke the color barrier in major league baseball. (Actually, he didn't. That distinction belongs to Moses Fleetwood Walker, but that's another story.) You likely know as well that Jackie was Rookie of the Year that season (1947). But here's the real challenge:

In the next season, another African-American player was offered Rookie of the Year but turned it down. Who?

"Satchel" Paige, forty-two years old at the time, with years of fabulously successful pitching behind him in the Negro Leagues. As he explained to the media, "[I] didn't know which year those gentlemen had in mind."

Now for another one you probably know. In the original *Star Trek* series on TV, there was only one female officer on the bridge, the communications officer, a lieutenant. She had a Swahili name. Lieutenant who? Right, Lieutenant Uhuru. Now the challenge: What does *Uhuru* mean?

It means "freedom" or "independence." Nichelle Nichols played Uhuru in the midst of all the male officers. Technically, however, there was one more female present. The voice of the *Enterprise*'s computer belonged to Majel Barrett, who also played the role of "Bones" McCoy's attractive, moony-eyed nurse several decks below.

Or try this one. If you shake a pair of these cubes in one hand and then roll them out onto a table, you are playing for the best payout rate in all forms of legalized gambling. The game? Of course, you're playing craps. Now, what form of legalized gambling has the *worst* payout rate?

This is how *Five-Minute Challenge* works. It's not the answer everyone knows that you're looking for. It's the *next* answer. What matters is not what Stanley said when he finally caught up with David Livingstone on the shores of Lake Tanganyika in 1871. It's Livingstone's reply! When the swallows come back to . . . well, you know where they come back to. The real question is: Where have they been? At the supermarket, when you have your eye out for that pricey, very special olive oil, you look for "extra virgin." *Five-Minute Challenge* wants to know, *what do you call the stuff after the wedding night?*

There are so many important questions in our fascinating world that deserve a brighter spot in the limelight. Who painted the *floor* of the Sistine Chapel, for example? Who was the *first* of the Mohicans? Did Whistler's mother ever stand up? We can't answer them all, but in the pages that follow, you do get the answers to one hundred of life's great stumpers.

Why five minutes? Because each challenge, or double-question, like "Who gave her mother forty whacks? *Did she really do it?*" is followed by a five-minute trivia journey into related subject matter. Moses Fleetwood Walker, for example, was an African American who preceded Jackie Robinson by some sixty-three years. Walker was a catcher for the Toledo Blue Stockings in 1884. They were a professional team (American Association) and Walker was a professional player, although he didn't stick it out as Jackie did, and by all accounts was not as accomplished a player. Jackie, incidentally, was not the first outstanding athlete from the Robinson family. A *Five-Minute Challenge* journey through the 1936 Olympics in Berlin describes older brother "Mack" Robinson, who finished four-tenths of a second behind Jesse Owens in the 200 meters and won the silver medal.

The swallows that come back to Capistrano, by the way, have been in Argentina. And the form of legalized gambling with the worst payout rate? Lotteries.

Q: Who was the first to orbit Earth in a spacecraft?

A: Yes, Russian cosmonaut Yuri Gagarin, in 1961.

The Challenge

Q: Who was the first to orbit Earth on a toilet seat?

A: **U.S. astronaut Pete Conrad**, in 1973. Conrad was on the can for ninety minutes, the time it took for the American *Skylab* space station to make one orbit of the planet. It was a specific project on his part, and he had his fellow astronauts verify the time, not to mention his activity. Gagarin's orbit was somewhat longer, 108 minutes, but since his *Vostok* did not have an *en suite*, it's likely he made a point of going ahead of time.

Although the American and Soviet space programs competed neck and neck for over thirty years, neither one came even close to solving outer-space potty problems in that time. In the early days, when short flights were the norm, the crews simply gritted their teeth. As flights lengthened, they were forced into designer diapers. But eventually the engineers on the ground had to come up with a working toilet for flights lasting over several days.

Not an easy task. Because of weightlessness, the stuff just won't plop! There's also the problem of storage (which, if nothing else, explains why giant pandas may never make it into orbit; on an average day, they go forty-eight times!). The U.S. Gemini program in the mid-1960s was especially plagued with the floating results of failed storage systems. How bad was it? Ask the navy frogman who opened the hatch of *Gemini 7* after it splashed down in the Pacific, and leaned in to say welcome back. He passed out and had to be resuscitated by his partner.

Q: These swallows must believe they're on to a good thing, for they keep coming back every year. They even have their own song: "When the Swallows Come Back to . . ." Come back to where?

A: Yes, Capistrano, in southern California.

The Challenge

Q: Where have they been?

A. **In Argentina.** The swallows leave there every March 19, and return on October 23, making a trip of over 6,000 miles (9,600 km) across four time zones.

Of course, the swallows pay no attention to time zones. Nor did Ferdinand Magellan's crew when they began the first round-the-world sail in September 1519. But when they were almost home, on July 9, 1522 – or was it July 10 – they met an outbound Portuguese ship off the Cape Verde Islands, and the two crews nearly came to blows over what day of the month it was. The Portuguese ship, only a few days out from its home port, was confident it was the tenth. This did not jibe, however, with the meticulous notes kept by Don Albo, one of Magellan's officers. Don Albo, never having attended a seminar on stress management, had scrupulously recorded the passing of each day of the journey for the previous three years, and so he knew for sure it was the ninth! Without realizing it, he had become the first European to establish the need for the international date line. If you travel west and go all the way around, you pick up one day.

Our planet's time-zoned day, in case you've been wondering, begins and ends in the Kingdom of Tonga, an island group just west of the date line, and in the Chukchi Peninsula, at the extreme eastern tip of Siberia. (The date line swings around this piece of Russian territory. They have enough troubles already without being on a different day.) Tonga used to be in the same time zone as nearby Fiji, but King Taufa'ahau Tupou IV switched to Tongan standard time in the 1970s. Neither Tonga nor Fiji has swallows that go anywhere near Capistrano.

Q: When the Vatican dropped this saint from the Roman Catholic calendar, dragons everywhere must have breathed a fiery sigh of relief. What is the name of this dragon-slaying saint?

A: Sure, Saint George, the knight in shining armor who saved a damsel in distress from a fire-breathing dragon.

The Challenge

Q: What is the name of the damsel?

A: **Sabra.**

Although the Vatican decided to delist George, so to speak, the Church of England has kept him front and center on its calendar. Most scholars generally agree there really was a George, that he was a Christian, and that he was put to death at Lydda, in Palestine, around the beginning of the third century. The dragon story comes from the Golden Legends, a good thousand years later.

In case you're not up on your legends, George wandered into the city of Sylene, in the province of Lybia, just as a local dragon had upgraded his daily requirements from two sheep to human beings; hence the plight of Sabra, who just happened to be the king's daughter. Into the breach leapt – or rather, rode – George, who elected to combine rescue with opportunity. At first, he only wounded the dragon. Then he took off Sabra's belt (This is not the opportunity we are referring to!) and used it to lead the dragon back to Sylene, where only after the citizens agreed to become Christians did he finish it off. George then married Sabra, and the dragon's carcass was carried away in four ox-carts. Why four? It's part of the legend!

If you are seeking a patron saint for your endeavors, St. George is already very busy. He's patron saint of England, Portugal, Germany, Genoa, Venice, and Aragon, as well as of boy scouts, farmers, and soldiers. St. Dunstan, on the other hand, is the patron saint of blacksmiths and lighthouse keepers, and therefore might conceivably have time for more responsibility.

6

Q: In 1995, on a busy night at the *Casino de Montréal*, a patron refused to get off her seat so paramedics could tend a heart attack victim who had fallen off the stool next to her. While this lady's name is unknown, the name of another gambler has been part of the language since 1762. On March 19 of that year, this British earl wanted to eat and still have one hand free to gamble, so his servants arranged a novel food item for him. He ate it in the early morning. We often have it at lunch. The food item?

A: Sure, the sandwich, named after John Montagu (1718–92), Fourth Earl of Sandwich.

The Challenge

Q: What kind of sandwich was it?

A. **Roast beef.** To be fair, "probably roast beef" is a more accurate answer. Most accounts say it was roast beef, although cheese, beef and cheese, and even ham come up. What is unchallenged is that the sandwich is attributed to Lord Montagu, even though the Romans had a similar snack two thousand years earlier. They ate it between meals and called it an *offula* (which could explain why we prefer "sandwich"). The Romans had ketchup too; they called it *liquamen*, and that word didn't catch on either.

The first written instance of the word "sandwich" appeared about 1770 in *Londres*, a travel publication by visiting Frenchman Pierre Grosley. His account makes clear that both the word and the idea had really caught on, but what is not clear is to what extent Montagu should get credit for this. Certainly His Lordship was well known, mostly for bribery, corruption, mismanagement, and membership in a not-so-secret society called the Mad Monks of Medmenham, who gathered in a ruined abbey to perform obscene parodies of Roman Catholic ritual. Montagu's dubious accomplishments include being First Lord of the Admiralty during the American Revolution – he did not perform well – having the Sandwich Islands (Hawaii) named after him by Captain James Cook, and being on the receiving end of one of the best-ever ripostes in the English language.

Having fallen out with John Wilkes, Lord Mayor of London (and one of the mad monks), the Earl once shouted at his former friend, "You, Wilkes, will either die on the gallows or from syphilis!"

Wilkes's unruffled reply: "That depends, my Lord, on whether I embrace your principles or your mistress."

Q: Arguably the best-known greeting of all time between two strangers, these words are attributed to Henry Morton Stanley. He addressed them to David Livingstone, on the shores of Lake Tanganyika on November 10, 1871. What did Stanley say?

A: Sure, "Doctor Livingstone, I presume?"

The Challenge

Q: What did Livingstone say in reply?

A: **"Yes."** Not exactly a bell-ringer, but poor Livingstone was probably not in the mood for sound bites. When the two met, he was in agony from malaria and dysentery, along with internal bleeding and arthritis. Not to mention semi-blindness from a branch that had whipped into his eyes, almost total deafness from rheumatic fever, and continuous pain in his left arm from a mauling by a lion. (Two years later, when his body was shipped back to England, it was the arm that confirmed Livingstone's identity. After his death in the Congo, two servants he'd rescued from slavery hung his body to dry, cured it in brandy and salt, and then carried it 1,000 miles [1,600 km] to the coast for shipment home.)

Stanley is the only reporter for the *New York Herald* ever to be elected to the British House of Commons (1895) and to be knighted (1899). Inspired by Livingstone, he became an important explorer of Africa in his own right and was in fact the first to complete a crossing of the continent: an epic 999-day journey, all within a few degrees of the equator. However, Stanley's request to be buried alongside Livingstone in Westminster Abbey was denied, even though he'd been born a British citizen (a workhouse foundling in Wales; he ran away to America in 1859).

The two men, according to the journals of both, had genuinely hit it off in Africa and spent several months exploring together. At the famous meeting, Stanley broke out a split of champagne to celebrate the occasion, and although Livingstone had been ordained by the teetotaling London Missionary Society some thirty years before, it's tempting to believe that his list of ailments was enough to grant him a dispensation for the occasion.

Q: It was way back in 1925 when American author Anita Loos popularized a widely held conviction about the hair color that gentlemen prefer in women. What is the title of Loos's book?

A: Sure, *Gentlemen Prefer Blondes*.

The Challenge

Q: Do they?

A: **No**, according to a scientific poll. A 1993 survey of 1,000 American males conducted for Harlequin, the premier publisher of romance novels, found that 31% picked women with brown hair while 29% opted for blondes. Another 18% went for black hair, 9% for red, and 3% for gray. Toting up these figures leaves a hundred guys who either had no preference or wisely kept their mouths shut. (The poll did not address the fact that blondes have more hair on their heads. They have about 140,000 strands, on average. That's 35,000 more than brunettes and 50,000 more than redheads.)

Hair follicles replace themselves approximately every fifty-six days. That's on your head. Elsewhere on your body, the process is slower, although science has also established that in the case of beards, blondes, who allegedly have more fun, also have more speed, for blond facial hair grows faster than that of other colors. It is unclear whether this slight anomaly led to any cases of pogonophobia (fear of beards) among the Russian nobility during Peter the Great's reign, but it's a reasonable assumption. In 1698, Peter imposed a beard tax, which he later modified so that offenders could be plucked clean, one hair at a time, with pincers.

Individual follicles, if you've ever tried to keep track, don't all grow at the same speed. About 10% of your hair is at rest at any one time, while the remainder is pushing you into a visit to the local tonsorial parlor.

Barbers (as if you didn't know) are notorious for doing all kinds of business on the side. As recently as 1975 in Yemen, for example, you could still get a circumcision with your haircut — not strictly "on the side," we'll grant you, but certainly entrepreneurial.

Q: Elephants trumpet, monkeys chatter and sometimes bark, Muscovy ducks hiss, and black-footed penguins bray. What do sheep do?

A: Right, they bleat. (For your notebook: pandas bleat too.)

The Challenge

Q: What do kangaroos do?

A: They cluck.

In a world where giraffes moan, weasels chirp, and oysters whistle, a clucking kangaroo should not raise any eyebrows. For the most part, these animal vocalizations are natural, not learned, so when ravens "cronk," it's not something they've picked up watching championship tennis.

Generally, we humans choose imitatively harmonic words for animal sounds, the extent of the lexicon usually varying with our level of affection for the beastie in question. Take cows, for instance. Despite their contribution to our well-being, we have only the rather pedestrian, albeit onomatopoeic, "moo." For those rare moments of bovine excitement, we have "bawl," and for even rarer moments of romantic surge, "low." One school of thought attributes the meagerness of this vocabulary to the fact that a cow belches and farts an average of forty-eight kilos of methane per year into the atmosphere. But the "dog factor" weakens this theory. *Canis familiaris* is equally distinguished for its flatulent proclivities, yet our words for its sounds go far beyond bark and growl, to include such refinements as yip, yap, yaup, yelp, whine, whimper, howl, tongue, bell, and, in moments of polysyllabic inspiration, ululate.

Whimpering saved the life of Rin Tin Tin (I), for he was found abandoned in a German trench in World War I. After that, and until he died in the arms of Jean Harlow in 1932, his security was assured without ever having to make another sound, for he starred in silent movies. Kangaroos, unfortunately, have never been much of a movie hit, although *Skippy, the Bush Kangaroo* was shown briefly on TV. Skippy never got any great lines (or plots). But he clucked a lot.

Q: Boxing takes place in a ring, football on a field; hockey is played in a rink, and ping pong on a table. On what is cricket played?

A: Yes, a pitch. The list goes on: basketball is played on a court, golf on a course (or links), and bowling on a lane in an alley.

The Challenge

Q: On what is kittenball played?

A: **On a diamond or field.** Kittenball is the original name for softball. Credit George Hancock, who first came up with the game – and the name – at the Farragut Boat Club of Chicago in 1887. The name changed to softball in 1926.

Kittenball called for a larger ball, a thinner bat, and a smaller playing area than baseball (a.k.a. hardball). Kittenball also re-established underhand pitching. In 1884, big league baseball had allowed the overhand pitch for the first time, creating a nightmare in the batter's box. At that time, only fifty feet (15.2 m) separated the mound from home plate, so that with the new rule, batting averages plunged and strikeout numbers skyrocketed. Hugh Daily, for example, a one-armed pitcher with Boston in the Union Association League, had 483 strikeouts! Catchers unable to handle the ball's speed – most caught bare-handed – compensated by backing up. Harry Decker helped them a lot when he introduced the "puff pillow mitt" but it was still not enough. Finally, in 1893, the pitching mound was moved back to sixty feet six inches (18.4 m), a distance which fans believe was an inspired choice but which in fact happened by chance. Baseball executives had agreed on sixty feet, but a mapping surveyor misread instructions and put 60' 6" on the official drawings.

Just as baseball grew from the English game of rounders, basketball too has an ancestry, for it is remarkably similar to an Aztec game, *ollamalitzli*. One tradition of *ollamalitzli*, not yet adopted by the NBA, allowed the player who dunked the winning layup to circle the crowd and claim all the spectators' clothing. Still another feature, one which dispassionate observers believe may yet be renewed in modern professional sport: The captain of the losing team was usually beheaded.

Q: You may not recognize this lady by her maiden name, Lisa Gherardini. Come to think of it, not that many people know her married name either: Mrs. Francesco del Giocondo. But everybody knows about her smile, thanks to Leonardo da Vinci, so that most of us know her as . . . ?

A: Indeed, Mona Lisa, possibly the most recognized face in the entire world.

The Challenge

Q: What's missing on that famous face?

A. **Eyebrows.** Some critics have suggested that the eyebrows have been lost through vigorous cleaning, but that would not explain why the wispy curls on her shoulders are intact. What is most likely is that da Vinci, or Lisa, or both, were just being true to the eyebrow-plucking fashion of the time.

Painted in Florence over a period from 1503 to 1507, the Mona Lisa has spent most of her life in France, except for planned international displays like the one in America in 1962. (She was appraised at $100 million for the trip.) Another exception was from 1911 to 1913, during an unscheduled visit to Italy, compliments of Vincenzo Perugia, an Italian carpenter who carried her out of the Louvre under his coat. Perugia was making vandal-resistant frames for the Louvre's collection, and stole the Mona Lisa as step one in a scam to sell "originals" to private collectors. During her absence, the scammers were able to make six "authenticated" sales in the U.S. alone. The project did no harm to the painting's fame, though. While Lisa was off the wall, so to speak, more people per day came to the Louvre to look at the blank space than had ever come to see the painting itself.

One story about Lisa Gherardini that just won't die is that her smile conceals dentures made by da Vinci out of teeth purloined from corpses. Although the practice was fairly common at the time, there is limited proof it really happened in her case. Greater certainty applies in the case of George Washington. He had a pair of dentures made of elk teeth set in lead, but apparently preferred a set made from the wood of a willow tree; poor color but not as heavy.

Q: On September 30, 1955, along Highway 66 near Paso Robles, California, a movie star was killed when his new silver Porsche Spyder 550, traveling at just under 90 mph (140 km/h) crashed into a black and white 1950 Ford Tudor. Who was driving the Porsche?

A: Right, actor/heartthrob/rebel James Dean.

The Challenge

Q: Who was driving the Ford?

A: **Donald Turnupseed.** He survived the crash, as did Dean's passenger, Rolf Weutherich.

The Porsche, it seems, wasn't fulfilled that day. Racing buff Troy McHenry bought the engine, installed it, and totaled his car in his very next race. Racer William Eschrid installed the drive train in his car. Next race? Same thing. A third collector bought the two front tires. Both blew out on the same trip. The California Highway Patrol turned the skin of the battered Porsche into a drive-safely-or-see-what-happens exhibit for teenagers. At a Sacramento high school it fell off its display pedestal and injured a student.

Dean and his Porsche make up what may be pop culture's best-known car crash, but there are other contenders. Karl Benz, for example (no explanation needed), was exhibiting a three-wheeled model of his new invention in Munich in 1885 and creamed it against a wall. At another, much sadder, demonstration in London, England, in 1896, a prototype horseless carriage built by the Anglo-French Motor Car Company killed spectator Bridget Driscoll, the world's first car death. Three years later, the first U.S. victim, Henry Bliss, stepped off a streetcar near Central Park and into the path of a car driven by Arthur Smith.

The only vehicle that ranks with Dean's Porsche as a jinx, however, is the phaeton in which Archduke Ferdinand and his wife were shot on June 28, 1914. Until 1926, when it was smashed once and for all, this car averaged one serious accident every two years and, excluding the royals, racked up a total of thirteen deaths and twenty serious injuries. Word must have got around too. From the time of Ferdinand's demise in Sarajevo, Serbia, to the end of the car in Cluj, Romania, it had fifteen different owners.

Q: We know Vladimir Ilyich Ulyanov today as V. I. Lenin. What was his party called?

A: Right, the Bolsheviks.

The Challenge

Q: What does *Bolshevik* mean?

A: "Majority." In 1903, at a meeting in Brussels, Lenin caused a split in the Marxist Russian Social Democratic Labor Party. The majority opted for his more radical and revolutionary approach, thus becoming the "majority-ites," or in Russian, Bolsheviks. It doesn't take a degree in political science to figure out that the Mensheviks, left behind in the split, were "minority-ites."

Although they differed widely in revolutionary philosophy, both Lenin and Yulii Tsederbaum, leader of the Mensheviks, had hemorrhoids. Karl Marx had them too. While it's tempting to view this affliction as the price one must pay for being a radical Communist – Marx once complained to Engels during the preparation of *Das Kapital*, "To finish, I must at least be able to sit down!" – the fact is that diverse, and clearly capitalistic, luminaries like Elizabeth Taylor, George Brett, Jimmy Carter, and Alfred the Great have also been members of the club. So was Napoleon, who was apparently too tender, at Waterloo, to spend much time astride the tall horse from which he customarily scanned the battlefield to modify strategy.

For some reason, the role of hemorrhoids in history has never been adequately explored, although such scholarly neglect may be owing to the fact that they are rarely, if ever, fatal. On the other hand, neither is falling off the Orient Express in pajamas, but when French president Paul Eugène Deschanel did precisely that in 1920, the event engendered a good deal more academic smirking than Napoleon's sore bottom ever did, despite the differences in outcome for the world.

The Emperor's favorite horse, by the way, was named Marengo. None of the biographies suggest Napoleon ever sat on him in pajamas.

Q: After the Wrights' achievement at Kitty Hawk, the most famous first in the annals of flight is a solo flight across the Atlantic. Like most people, you may have trouble spelling the last name of the pilot, but you certainly know who he is. His identity?

A: Right, Lindbergh. Charles Augustus Lindbergh, on May 20–21, 1927, in the *Spirit of Saint Louis* (called that, but built in San Diego; Wrong-Way Corrigan was one of the builders). Lindbergh was not the first to fly across the Atlantic, however. If you count airship crews, he was actually the eighty-first!

The Challenge

Q: Who was first?

A: **Albert Read**, and a crew of five. British airmen John Alcock and Arthur Brown were the first to fly across *non-stop*. They flew from Newfoundland to Ireland on June 14–15, 1919. Read had crossed a month earlier, but not non-stop. He and his crew went from Newfoundland to Portugal, but made a pit stop in the Azores.

The slice of pedantry above is typical of the who-was-first squabbles that prevail in aviation history. For example, thirteen years before Kitty Hawk, on October 9, 1890, Frenchman Clement Ader took off and flew his aircraft, the *Eole*, for 164 feet (50 m) entirely under its own power (a light-weight steam engine). Yet fans of the Wrights-were-first movement — who clearly have the media on their side — describe Ader's achievement as a "hop" and Orville's first shot (120 feet [36.6 m]) as a "flight." Go figure.

The following aviation firsts, however, have never been challenged:

- First emergency use of an ejection seat: Luftwaffe Major Rudolf Schenk in a Heinkel 280, January 13, 1942.
- First aerial propaganda raid: the Italian *Servizi Aeronautici* over Libya, January 15, 1912. Leaflets promised a gold coin and a sack of barley to each Turkish soldier who surrendered.
- First free flight bags: KLM on the Amsterdam–Jakarta route, April 1935, but you had to go the whole route to get one.
- First in-flight meals: pre-packed box lunches on the London–Paris run by Handley Page Transport on October 11, 1919. Passengers had to pay three shillings.
- First airplane toilet: the Russian passenger transport *Russki Vitiaz*, test flown (and flushed) on May 13, 1913.

Q: Mr. Ed, Wilbur's talking palomino on the TV sitcom of the same name, won four consecutive PATSY Awards, and even had his own theme song, which began, "A horse is a . . ." A horse is a what?

A: Yes, a horse.

The Challenge

Q: If a horse is a horse, then what is a toad?

A. **A frog.** Not that this should cause you any stress, but a toad is indeed a type of frog. Fortunately, there are some lifestyle differences which, in moments of crisis, can be used to distinguish the two. Toads lay eggs in strings, for example, whereas frogs tend to deposit theirs in clumps. As well, toads have thicker skin, thicker soles, and, according to a carefully constructed experiment by Canadian biologists, tend to be right-handed (well, right-footed), unlike most other non-human animals, which seem to be evenly distributed in right-left preference. Nose-to-nose (i.e., you and the frog – or toad), it's harder to make distinctions, especially if they are eating, for neither frogs nor toads eat with their eyes open. What they do is close their eyes while swallowing and push the eyeballs down against the roof of the mouth. This helps force food down into the stomach. All in all, it's quite an effective process, given that the prey being swallowed is usually tied up and surrounded by the frog's – or toad's – very long and sticky tongue.

Both creatures are members of the order Anura (about 3,500 species), and over the years, they have managed to attract some interesting mythology, the toad-wart tradition being among the most popular. For drama, however, Cambodia gets top prize. In 1972, the Khmer Rouge ordered its armed forces to fire at the moon during an eclipse in order to save it from the monster frog, Reahou. When the smoke cleared, there were over fifty casualties and two civilians had been killed. But the moon was saved.

Toads are members of the family Bufonidae. Some frogs are of the family Ranidae. Mr. Boynton, the biology teacher on the *Our Miss Brooks* show, called his frog MacDougal. He didn't have a toad.

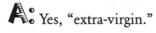

Q: Right beside the pure olive oil at your local supermarket is another type of olive oil which is a lot more expensive. What is this olive oil called?

A: Yes, "extra-virgin."

The Challenge

Q: What do you call it after the wedding night?

A: "Extra-virgin." Once it becomes extra-virgin it stays that way no matter what happens to it.

Making extra-virgin oil is costly, for the oil must contain less than 1% oleic acid and that's not easy to achieve. First of all, the olives are handpicked, since mechanical harvesters can bruise the fruit and don't discriminate for peak ripeness. The selected olives are dried for a few days before being cold-pressed into a paste, which is then led through a few more processes before the product is ready. The key, we are told, is gentleness and heat. Not enough of the former and too much of the latter will apparently squeeze the "extra" out of the virginity, leaving plain old "virgin" olive oil, or even worse, the next grade down, "pure." Incidentally, the term "light" in the case of olive oil refers neither to a standard nor to a calorie count. Olive oil is straight fat, whether it's light, fine, pure, virgin, or a street-corner strumpet.

All this fuss, naturally, takes a bit of time, and that, to a large extent, accounts for the extra cost. On the plus side, extra-virgin oil tends to outlive other grades before turning rancid. Science has yet to work out whether such longevity applies in other forms of nature, although British biologists in the 1970s discovered that female mice live longer if they remain *hymen intacta*, although female cats do not. Unfortunately, research data for humans is so difficult to obtain that seekers after truth are forced to extrapolate from known cases: Isaac Newton, for example. A life-long virgin, he lived to eighty-five at a time when average life expectancy was about half that. Victorian poet Alfred Tennyson courted Emily Sellwood for fourteen years, and did not lose his virginity until he married her at age forty-one. He lived for another forty-two years.

Q: What Roman emperor, a noted arsonist, won a gold medal in the 66 Olympic games?

A: Sure, Nero.

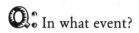

The Challenge

Q: In what event?

A: **The chariot race.** Like the 100-meter dash of the modern games, the chariot race was a "biggie," so it was important that the Emperor win, especially since he'd brought a personal retinue of 5,000 bodyguards and servants with him as a cheering section — not that local citizens were stupid enough to cheer for anyone else. Nero entered several events (won them all) and even made up some on the spot (won them too), but the chariot race was the most farcical of all. He lost control of his horses, so the race was stopped until his grooms were able to help him regroup and regain the lead.

Supporters of today's Olympic Games wince visibly when reminded of just how the original games went to pot. The first recorded game, in 776 B.C., was a Greek-only, one-event affair, a foot race. As the idea grew, more races, javelin throwing, discus, boxing and wrestling, and a pentathlon were added, but with growth, the purity and amateurism diminished. A 45,000-seat stadium was built (no women allowed; the penalty for sneaking in was to be thrown off a nearby cliff). Gymnasia were put up, along with baths and shrines, so that athletes could train, relax, and pray. In 776, the race had been won by a local cook, but soon the larger cities were hiring professionals, especially to compete in the new pancratium event, a fight to the finish which allowed everything except biting and eye-gouging. Even though the games had become somewhat of a joke by Nero's time, they hung on until 394, when Emperor Theodosius I canceled them as totally commercialized, non-amateur, and corrupt.

Nero, you might be interested to know, did not carry the Olympic Torch despite his alleged love of flame. The torch didn't feature until 1936, in Berlin.

Q: How many zeroes are there in a trillion?

A: Right, twelve. But you get points too, if you said eighteen. This is one of those cross-cultural confusions, because in England, twelve zeroes gets you only a billion; it takes eighteen to make a trillion there.

The Challenge

Q: There is international agreement on this one: How many zeroes in a postillion?

A: **None.** A postillion (or postilion) is the rider on the near horse of the leading pair pulling a coach. If you have been reincarnated from 1559, and happened to be in London during January of that year, you probably saw a postillion with Elizabeth I's coronation coach. At the time, you would not have been fretting over billions and trillions, because neither idea had yet worked its way into European thought. Million came in around 1300. Before that, the largest word was myriad, Greek for 10,000. Generally, the Arabic numerals we know and love (and hate) weren't fully accepted in Europe until the eighteenth century.

The billion/trillion difference is typical of the vocabulary preferences that bug mathematicians. The British are still not keen about the googol (1 followed by 100 zeroes), which American Edward Kasner coined in the early twentieth century (soon followed by the googolplex: 1 followed by 10-to-the-power-100 zeroes). It seems that number geeks at Oxford and Cambridge get their warm fuzzies from more Latinate terms like quintoquadagintillion (1 followed by 138 zeroes), which Charles Babbage dreamed up in 1854.

Mathematicians are unanimous on prime numbers, though (numbers that can be divided only by themselves and 1). There are infinitely many primes. In 1971, a computer calculated one that is 6,002 digits long. In 1996, a Cray T94 System research team in Chippewa Falls, Wisconsin, cranked out a prime of 378,632 digits, a number which, printed out in a standard typesize, would fill twelve newspaper pages! (Despite this achievement in their very midst, residents of Chippewa Falls still prefer ice-fishing.)

The near horse, by the way, is the one on the left. The one on the right is the off horse. This matters to postillions.

Q: In the early part of the twentieth century, a steamship line commissioned three "Olympic class" passenger liners. The first was the *Olympic* (hence the name of the class). The second, almost identical, was the *Titanic*. The third was the *Britannic*. What was the name of this steamship line?

A: Right, the White Star line.

The Challenge

Q: Only one of these three ships made it to the scrapyard on her own. Which one?

A. **The *Olympic*.**

The *Britannic* (originally called the *Gigantic*, but that was changed after April 15, 1912) blew up in 1916 and went down in fifty-five minutes, three times faster than the *Titanic*.

The *Olympic*, launched in 1910, acquired the nickname "Old Reliable" before she was scrapped in 1934, not so much as a poor-taste dig at her sisters as because she was indeed a trooper. In 1911, she collided with the British cruiser *Hawke* but sailed away intact. (Her captain on that occasion was E. J. Smith, who commanded the *Titanic* a year later.) She survived four submarine attacks in World War I. During the last one, she sank the sub. After the war she went into trans-Atlantic service and logged thousands of crossings. Even her pre-scrap journey was eventful, for in dense fog she survived one last collision. (The other ship didn't.)

One other White Star survivor, who never managed to acquire a handle like "Old Reliable," even though she may have deserved it, was Violet Jessup. She survived the sinking of the *Titanic* and the blowup of the *Britannic*. And she was aboard the *Olympic* when it hit the *Hawke*!

While the late Ms. Jessup can thus lay reasonable claim to a record for survival, the record for plain spooky, when it comes to marine disasters, goes to three different people named Hugh Williams. On December 5, 1664, in the Menai Strait in North Wales, a ferry sank with eighty-one passengers aboard. The lone survivor was a man named Hugh Williams. On December 5, 1785, another ferry sank in the Menai Strait. Of the sixty-three aboard, the only survivor was named Hugh Williams. Then again in 1860, again on December 5, and again in the Menai Strait, a ferry sank with twenty passengers aboard. One person made it to shore: Hugh Williams.

Q: Of all James Abbott McNeill Whistler's paintings, one is far better known than any other. Who was the model for this famous piece?

A: Sure, Whistler's mother.

The Challenge

Q: What is the title of the painting?

A: *Arrangement in Gray and Black, No. 1: Portrait of the Artist's Mother.*

Anna has been called "America's most famous mother," but Whistler, like everyone else who came near, found her pretty hard to take. Without her immediate presence, however, James Whistler might never have made it as an artist – or as anything else. He had both an inheritance and a problem concentrating.

After being kicked out of West Point, Whistler went to Paris at age twenty-one to study painting. But he never bothered to go to the lessons arranged for him, turning instead to the initial development of a modest string of illegitimate children. At age twenty-nine, he seemed to be settling down with his drop-dead gorgeous mistress/model, Joanne Hiffernan, when Anna showed up, got rid of Joanne, and took over. That Whistler was enthusiastic about the new arrangement is doubtful, for both his artistic and his progenerative output dropped significantly. The famous painting came about because a model failed to show one day in 1871, and he idly turned to his mother as a fallback choice.

When Anna's health declined and she was no longer able to monitor him with the necessary vigor, Whistler took up where he left off, fathering two more children and taking to eccentricities somewhat unusual even for Paris. Like wearing red pumps with pink bows. He also went bankrupt.

To the end, Whistler scoffed at critics who found layers of emotion in the portrait of his mother, maintaining that on the contrary, it contained no more than was implied by the title. Yet it's clear he must have picked up some of Anna's traits, for he once sued John Ruskin over a negative review. He is also the author, in 1890, of *The Gentle Art of Making Enemies*.

Q: Near the end of World War II, a small group of Japanese pilots both fascinated and frightened the Allies by sacrificing themselves and their aircraft in suicidal dives, mostly against ships. What were these pilots called?

A: Yes, kamikaze pilots.

The Challenge

Q: What does *kamikaze* mean?

A: "Divine wind." In 1274, and again in 1281, freak (or divine) winds destroyed huge armadas sent by Kublai Khan, grandson of Genghis, to conquer Japan. The Mongols, who by land had conquered everything from China to Russia, Hungary, Turkey, and Persia, never ever managed to get across the 125-mile (200-km) Tsushima Strait to Japan. Kublai was stopped in Burma too, in 1287, where his cavalry was spooked when it met elephants for the first time. Far less successful in stopping the Mongols was Pope Innocent IV. With no faith at all in either elephants or kamikazes, he sent a sixty-year-old Franciscan friar, Giovanni da Pian del Carpini, deep into Asia with an offer of baptism to then Mongol leader Guyuk Khan (another Genghis grandson). Guyuk's guffaws were a surprise to absolutely no one except Innocent, and about all the mission accomplished was to have Carpini become the first European to cross into Asia by land, ahead of Marco Polo by twenty-six years.

The virtually unstoppable Mongols had very advanced weaponry. They had armor-piercing arrows, they used pontoon bridges, and they had surveyor-style instruments to support their "artillery," particularly the stone-heaving mangonel, which leveled out any advantage offered by a fortress.

Perhaps inspired by the Mongols' creativity, Allied Command in 1943 authorized a weapons experiment wherein small flash bombs were attached to live bats. The intent was to release them over German cities. By 1945, when the experiment was abandoned, the U.S. Army Corps had several million bats ready to go. According to declassified reports, the final decision on this already dubious venture was taken when a flock of armed bats – perhaps undertrained – destroyed an aircraft hangar and a general's car.

Q: Of Beethoven's nine symphonies, only the last one has a choral component. The final movement is a musical setting for a poem. What is the poem?

A: Yes, "Ode to Joy," sometimes even used as the title of Beethoven's Symphony no. 9 in D Major.

The Challenge

Q: Who wrote the poem?

A: **Friedrich von Schiller** (1759–1805), in Germany, known almost as well as Beethoven. Had Schiller knuckled under to the Duke of Wurttemburg in 1781, no one would ever have heard of him. He was a surgeon in the Duke's army and went AWOL to see the opening of his first play. As punishment, the Duke sentenced Schiller to write nothing but medical treatises, but in a display of Beethoven-like behavior, the young doctor told the Duke where to get off, and spent the next ten years wandering about – and becoming famous.

Beethoven treated his royal sponsors more dramatically, one of the more notable examples being his attack of Prince Lichnowsky with a chair. To be fair, Beethoven didn't discriminate by social status. He beat up on maids, servants, waiters, his family, his publisher, and musicians of all stripes and quality. Even cows. At Gneixendorf, where he conceived the exquisitely beautiful Pastoral Symphony, a herdsman complained to authorities that Beethoven made his cattle run away! Beethoven's table manners included spitting conspicuously and using the closest item available for a toothpick.

It would have been interesting to see Beethoven's reaction had he been present on Good Friday, 1988, for a performance of his *Missa Solemnis* by the Ealing Choral Society. In the hush before the final bars, the entrance door slammed and a figure in helmet, boots, and chains clanked up the center aisle, terrifying the audience, performers, and conductor, Professor James Gaddarn. It turned out that an undergraduate with a part-time job delivering kissograms had blundered into the wrong hall. After the mix-up was sorted out, he clumped back out and the music resumed. All present agreed the event was a personal first. Likely for Beethoven too.

Q: In 1893, the sixteenth earl of Derby paid tribute to the popularity of ice hockey by donating a trophy that has come to represent the sport's pinnacle of success. What's the name of the trophy?

A: Of course, the Stanley Cup, premier emblem of professional hockey. Frederick Arthur, Baron Stanley of Preston, was governor-general of Canada when he donated the cup-shaped silver bowl as a prize for the best hockey team in the country.

The Challenge

Q: It's officially the Stanley Cup now, but that's not what Lord Stanley called it. What name did he give the prize?

A: **The Dominion Hockey Challenge Cup.** Montreal heads the list of cup winners, with six teams: the Amateur Athletic Association (the first ever to win), the Victorias, the Shamrocks, the Wanderers, the Canadiens (who first won in 1916), and the Maroons. Toronto has had four winners: the Blue Shirts, the Arenas, and the St. Patricks, all victorious before the present-day Maple Leafs won it for the first time in 1932.

The cup was very much an amateurs' challenge at first, as the 1906 victory of the Kenora Thistles attests. There's also the team from Dawson City, Yukon, which was outscored 32–4 in the 1905 series after traveling 3,800 miles (6,400 km) by dogsled, ship, and train to take on the Ottawa Silver Seven. The first U.S. team to win was the Seattle Metropolitans in 1917. They were doing well again in 1919 when the series was canceled – the only time in its history – because of the Spanish flu pandemic.

The trophy has had a wonderfully colorful history. It has been taken home for a barbecue (by Guy Lafleur of the Canadiens in 1979), used as a flowerpot (by the wife of the Ottawa Silver Seven's photographer; she had no idea what it was and just went ahead on a reasonable assumption), stolen from Chicago Stadium (in 1961, by a Canadiens fan who couldn't bear to see it there), and left at the side of the road (in 1924, when players got out to change a tire).

The Stanley Cup series is the only professional team championship event in North America at the end of which all players on both sides line up to shake hands. This is a tradition which Lord Stanley wanted to reinforce. Unfortunately, he never got to see a Stanley Cup game. He was called back to England before the 1893 series and never came back to Canada.

◁ **22** ▷

Q: Someone is crying, but you suspect that the tears are not genuine. Now, you might say that he or she is being "falsely lachrymose," or you might call the display an "insincere threnody." But you can be more assured of being understood if you simply say he or she is shedding a particular kind of tears. What kind?

A: Yes, crocodile tears.

The Challenge

Q: To be sure, the question cries out, do crocodiles shed tears?

A: **Yes and no.** Crocodiles do not have tear glands, but a tear-like lubricant runs from the eyes into the mouth when they swallow prey. Apparently this helps things slide down the chute.

The origin of the phrase "crocodile tears" is often attributed to Roman naturalist Pliny the Elder (A.D. 23–79), who had a reputation for getting extremely close to make careful observations. (That's how he got buried by lava from Mount Vesuvius.) More likely, the myth comes from fifteenth-century travelers like Edward Topsell, who wrote that "such is the nature of the crocodile that, to get a man within his danger, he will sob, sigh and weep as though he were in extremity, but suddenly he destroyeth him." Topsell also advised potential victims to scare off a crocodile by maintaining a steady gaze with the right eye and winking with the left.

Empiricists who would like to evaluate Topsell's advice should test it first on alligators; they are less aggressive than crocodiles. Even better would be the still gentler, narrow-snouted gharial of southern Asia. (It's also spelled gairial and gavial, but if you spot one after falling out of your canoe, spelling may not be your first consideration.) Also in the mix, found in South and Central America, is the caiman — or cayman. (For reptiles with shockingly small brains, members of the order Crocodilia are awfully persnickety about spelling.)

Alligators have a shorter, broader snout than crocodiles, but the best way to distinguish the two is to note the fourth tooth from the front on both sides of the lower jaw. On alligators it's hidden when the jaws are closed; on crocodiles it sticks out. To do this, needless to say, you may have to get as close as Pliny the Elder, so be sure of your footing.

Q: There's a number missing on the dial of North American television sets. What number is that?

A: Yes, 1. There's no Channel 1 (44 to 50 MHz).

The Challenge

Q: There's a letter missing on our telephone pads too. (OK, in addition to Z, there's a letter missing.) What's that letter?

A: **Q.** When human operators were replaced by telephone dials, the numbers 1 and 0 were set aside for special "flag" functions like dialing 1 for long distance. With eight numbers (2–9) left, in order to assign three letters per number, only twenty-four of the alphabet's twenty-six letters were needed; two letters had to go. Z was an easy drop, but for the other choice, Q had to compete with X for this distinction.

TV had a Channel 1 briefly, in 1945, but then the frequency was given over to mobile radios, perhaps so that CBers could try to match the idiot box for intellectual challenge. Not too big a task, given stats like this: On January 20, 1953, forty-four million people were tuned to *I Love Lucy* for the episode "Lucy Goes to the Hospital" (to have a baby). At the same time, on another channel, only twenty-seven million watched Dwight D. Eisenhower's presidential inauguration. Still, it could be that the majority was demonstrating an insight Ike himself appreciated, for he once said he could "think of nothing more boring than . . . for a whole half hour, looking at my face on a television screen."

For the record, Eisenhower's swearing-in was not carried live in Cambodia. It's possible they were too busy working on a telephone dial design at the time, for the Cambodian alphabet has seventy-two letters. The Hebridean island of Lewis missed it too, because they didn't have TV. Or dial telephones. But they had a one-of-a-kind telephone directory. Since there were so many identical names on Lewis, the directory used nicknames. One of the male McLeods, for example, was Dolly Droggy, and one of the Gileses was Bimbo. Alex Murray was Eve.

Because it receives BBC Television, Lewis Island has a Channel 1.

Q: Washington Irving, writing in 1809 under the name of Diedrich Knickerbocker, helped popularize the idea of Santa Claus flying through the air with presents. Cartoonist Thomas Nash established the white-bearded, red-suited image in 1863. And Clement C. Moore gave us the big poem in 1822. Can you recite the poem's first few lines?

A: "'Twas the night before Christmas,
And all through the house,
Not a creature was stirring –
Not even a mouse!"

The Challenge

Q: What is the title of this poem?

A: **"A Visit from St. Nicholas."** The poem never once says "Santa Claus." The name only came into popular use in Nash's time. Like Irving's St. Nick, Moore's is a jolly old fellow who skims over the treetops and lands on roofs. But Irving's man used a wagon. And there was no sliding down the chimney with the presents either; his guy dropped them down!

You are probably aware that there really was a Saint Nicholas. He's patron saint of Russia, even though he was from Turkey. But that's all right: Saint Patrick isn't Irish either. In the face of such displacement, it's encouraging to know that there really was a Good King Wenceslaus. Not only that, he's the patron saint of the Czech Republic, and is really from there (Bohemia). Still, nothing's perfect. Wenceslaus went out "while the snow lay round about," on the Feast of Stephen. That's a day *after* Christmas. And he was never really a king. Although in line for the throne, Wenceslaus was murdered by his brother, Boleslaw, with some help from their mother, in 935.

Unlike St. Nick's delivery system, the gold, frankincense, and myrrh in "We Three Kings" arrives via quite believable transport, but the accuracy of the carol may face other challenges. Biblical scholars contend that the "gold" was really high-grade frankincense, at the time worth more than the metal. Frankincense is a resin. So is myrrh (a.k.a. sweet cicely). On balance, though, the song's composer was probably wise not to work a line like "high-quality resin, regular-grade resin, and sweet cicely" into the chorus.

Frankincense from Oman sells for about two dollars an ounce today. The best myrrh is from Yemen. It's used for perfume, cooking, and embalming, and goes for about five dollars. Compare that with a good camel, which in both countries will fetch up to $2,000–$3,000.

25

Q: A centuries-old expression describing cramped quarters begins, "No room to swing a . . ." Swing a what?

A: Sure, a cat.

The Challenge

Q: What is a "cat" in this expression?

A: **A whip.** A "cat" left claw-like scars on the back of anyone who was flogged, especially if it had barbs at the end — typically the case in the British navy.

The erect penis of a tomcat also has such barbs, and there is a theory that after a close study of cats in the act of copulation, the military was inspired to modify its whips accordingly. This hypothesis weakens, however, in the face of chronology. The hooks on a male cat's *organus erectus* were not discovered (by humans, anyway) until the twentieth century. The flogging of sailors, on the other hand, was abolished in 1881, sixty years after Parliament had granted horses and dogs the same exemption. Female cats, properly called "queens," by the way — mongrel cats are "moggies" — are so completely undeterred by the prospect of entertaining barbed toms, that it is not uncommon for them to conceive a litter with the help of several different males at the same time. Although other words may spring to mind, the correct term for this type of group adventure is "superfecundation."

Opportunity for superfecundation must have been abundant in the home of Florence Nightingale, for she kept up to sixty cats, each named after a dignitary like Bismarck or Disraeli. According to *The Complete Book of Pet Names*, such inspired handles don't even make the outer edges of popularity with modern cat owners. The ranking tickets today are Fluffy, Boots, Tiger, Smokey, and Kitty.

Cats are pacers, which accounts for their unusual walking rhythm. According to Frédéric Chopin, this rhythm inspired his Waltz no. 3 in F, when a cat walked across his piano. Since cats share this peculiar ambulatory style with camels and giraffes, one cannot help wondering what Chopin might have written had one of these been in his studio.

Q: Of the three most popular field games played with a ball and a club, only one can be played in the average back yard. What game is that?

A: Indeed, croquet. The other two, polo and golf, take up too much space. (So does shinty, a club and ball game which most people outside Scotland have never heard of. If played in the traditional Scottish manner, shinty can take up a whole county.)

The Challenge

Q: Polo is played on a field and golf on a course. What is croquet played on?

A: **A court.** Early on in *Croquet: Its Principles and Rules*, published by Milton Bradley in 1871, author A. Rover issues a sharp warning: "Keep your temper . . ." This suggests that the image of croquet as a genteel, white clothing and cucumber sandwiches affair may not be accurate. Also, Rover continues with ". . . and remember when your turn comes," an indication that in his day, players may well have had more than the sheer joy of victory in mind. Inasmuch as croquet was about the only physical sport that social customs of the period allowed both sexes to play together, one can see the reasoning behind Rover's advice. As it turned out, his admonitions weren't strong enough for the city of Boston, where croquet was banned in the late 1890s.

Typically, enthusiasts of croquet have been those who can afford to be somewhat self-indulgent. The game was big in Hollywood in the 1920s and 1930s, with moguls like Darryl Zanuck and Sam Goldwyn arranging regular Sunday matches. Harpo Marx had a separate air-conditioned bedroom to store his equipment. Averell Harriman, former U.S. ambassador to the U.S.S.R. (1943–46), is said to have made the installation of a court a precondition of his acceptance of the Moscow post. No less a light than Rutherford B. Hayes, while he was president, allocated six dollars from the treasury for the purchase of "good quality croquet balls."

Croquet was a medal sport in the 1904 Olympics (gold to the U.S.). So was golf (gold to Canada). Polo has never made it. However, polo was a favorite sport of Genghis Khan's, who was given to arranging games using the skulls of defeated generals instead of balls, which just shows that if you have a conquering army and a big enough back yard, you don't need the Olympics.

27

Q: There's something utterly delicious about proving the experts wrong. Case in point: the New York *Tribune*'s pronouncement of Puccini's *La Boheme* as "silly and inconsequential" in its review of the opera's New York opening. The *Trib* also labeled *Porgy and Bess* "sure-fire rubbish" thirty-five years later. Then there are the Decca Recording Company executives whose memo in 1962 rejected four young musicians from Liverpool this way: "We don't like their sound. Groups of guitars are on the way out." What rock and roll group was this memo turning down?

A: Of course, the Beatles. (Decca was not alone. The Beatles were also rejected by Pye, Columbia, and HMV.)

The Challenge

Q: In 1955, Elvis Presley and the Blue Moon Boys, his original backup group, auditioned for a widely syndicated, coast-to-coast amateur show but, like the Beatles, were rejected. What show?

A: *Arthur Godfrey's Talent Scouts.* Just months later, Presley broke into *Billboard* magazine's top ten (with "Heartbreak Hotel") and stayed there with his next twenty-nine releases. The thirtieth, "One Broken Heart for Sale," peaked at number eleven in 1963. By this time, Godfrey's show was no longer on the air.

Not that Godfrey's staff or the Decca executives were alone out there on the limb. In 1957, Frank Sinatra was quoted thus: "[Rock and roll is] phony and false . . . written and played for the most part by cretinous goons." A few years later, he paid Presley a fortune to sing for six minutes on a TV special. Rock and roll seemed to push other noted authorities into the pronouncement act too. Evangelist Billy Graham broke a personal rule in February 1964 – he watched TV on a Sunday – in order to see the Beatles on the *Ed Sullivan Show*, and immediately declared them a passing fad. The Beatles flubbed their lyrics that night, but it's difficult to know whether Graham was influenced by that.

The talent for being dead wrong seems to be one of those wonderfully human traits that grow out of misunderstanding, misinformation, and haste – which may explain why media people so often have to eat their words. Everyone knows the *Chicago Tribune*'s famous "Dewey Defeats Truman" headline from 1948. Not as well known, although it should be, is the *Lancashire Evening Post*'s headline on the sinking of the Titanic: "All the Passengers Are Safe." Also worthy of mention, from the early 1960s: "And for the tourist who really wants to get away from it all – safaris in Vietnam" (*Newsweek*), and "Sterility May Be Inherited" (*Pacific Rural News*).

28

Q: Of these rulers, Charlemagne, Julius Caesar, Alexander the Great, and David, the slayer of Goliath, only one was never actually a king. Which one?

A: Indeed, Julius Caesar. He was a quaestor, a curule aedile, and a pontifex maximus, as well as a praetor, propraetor, consul, and proconsul, among other things, but never a king, even though he turned down an offer just a month before his assassination.

The Challenge

Q: Other than in a history book, gallery, or museum, where is the only place you will find Charlemagne, Caesar, David, and Alexander together?

A: **In a deck of playing cards.** In Western countries, Charlemagne is the model for the king of hearts, David for spades; Alexander is clubs and Caesar diamonds.

Of these, only Alexander and Charlemagne ever became known as "Great," even though attaching descriptive titles to kings is a centuries-old tradition. The many European kings named Charles or Louis, for example, have included a Bold, a Wise, and a Fair, along with a Noble, a Pious, and a Well Beloved. And a Simple, a Bald, a Fat, a Quarreler, and a Sluggard. Charlemagne's own father was Pepin the Short – he was shorter than his own sword – and Charlemagne's mother was Bertha of the Big Foot. Russia has had Greats – and a Terrible. Louis the Strict once reigned in southern Germany. In 878, Germany's Charles the Bald got into a war with Spain's Wilfrid the Hairy. Also Spanish was Joanna the Mad, daughter of Columbus's sponsors, Ferdinand and Isabella. Turkey had a Suleiman the Magnificent (a Western sobriquet; his own people called him the Lawmaker). They also had a Selim the Grim and a Selim the Sot. In Britain, there was both praising and sneering too: Alfred the Great, Edward the Confessor, and Richard Lionheart line up with Aethelred (II) the Unready, Richard (III) Crookback, and Silly Billy (William IV).

You need not be a historian to figure out that names don't always reflect reality. For centuries, it was customary in France to set fire to a cage full of live cats at the annual festival of John the Baptist. This gross-out became royal in 1648 when Louis XIV applied the match. And he was the Sun King! Things were no different across the Channel, where a wicker effigy of Pope Paul IV was filled with live cats and burned at Elizabeth I's coronation. She was called Good Queen Bess.

29

Q: What does a barometer measure?

A: Correct, atmospheric pressure.

The Challenge

Q: What does an ancroid barometer measure?

A: Same Thing. The earliest form of barometer was devised in 1643 by Evangelista Torricelli, a colleague of Galileo. (Torricelli also built a microscope and a form of cycloid; not bad for a blind person.) His barometer used a bowl and a tube filled with mercury. The aneroid type is a metal box containing a vacuum. Both devices work well but the aneroid is usually preferred, especially if the technicians are a bit clumsy. Barometers, anemometers (wind velocity), pluviometers (rainfall), and hygrometers (humidity) are important instruments for gathering data on events like a circular storm – called "hurricane" in the Atlantic, "typhoon" in the North Pacific, and "cyclone" in the South Pacific and Indian Oceans. A tornado is a circular storm too. None of these storms earns its respective classification until the wind gets up to 74 mph. (That's about 120 km/h if you're metrically inclined, but chances are that measurement system preference will be the last thing on your mind if you happen to encounter a gale of this strength.)

The worst circular storm ever recorded, in terms of human casualties, was off Bangladesh in November 1970. Bangladesh also endured the worst-ever tornado, in 1989. The same country also gets hit by tsunamis. Contrary to popular belief, tsunamis are not tidal waves, but this nicety did not deter a doctoral student at Hong Kong University in the 1980s, who calculated that if the entire population of China were to jump up and down synchronistically, the resulting vibrations would generate a wave high enough to reach the middle of the North American continent. We were unable to discover whether her investigations included the impact this wave would have on China.

30

Q: Hardly anyone knew Jean François Gravelet until he crossed Niagara Falls in 1859 under the name of Blondin. After that, everyone knew who he was. How did the great Blondin cross Niagara Falls?

A: Right, on a tightrope. For the sake of historical precision, he did it on 1,300 feet of two-inch manila (or, if you prefer, 396.24 m x 50.8 mm). Blondin crossed from the U.S. side to the Canadian in fifteen minutes and went back in just seven. The first time was longer because he paused in mid-manila to do some stunts.

The Challenge

Q: How did teenager Homan Walsh cross Niagara in 1848?

A: With a kite. Walsh won a contest organized as the first step in building a suspension bridge. From the lip of the Niagara River gorge at Lewiston, NY, his kite was the first to snag on a tree over at Queenston, Ontario. His string was then used to drag a rope across, then larger ropes, until an iron cable could be strung between two wooden towers.

Within a year, Niagara had a powerful tourist draw to go with the falls: the world's first successful railway suspension bridge. Even before this, shoreline railroads on both sides had been lugging in thousands of sightseers, including luminaries like President Martin Van Buren, in 1838. His trip was among the more memorable, because the train fell off the track. Van Buren wasn't hurt, and even helped push his car back onto the rails.

As a major atttraction, however, nothing and no one approached Blondin. Huge crowds gathered to watch this master showman walk across, dance, push a wheelbarrow, take a stove out and cook on it, stand on his head, cross on stilts, hang upside-down, and get rich in the process. Not bad for an entertainer who couldn't afford the rope for his first crossing. Professionally, Blondin was a funambulist, a term not to be confused with funicular, which is a cable railway on a steep incline. (There is one of these today on the Canadian side at Niagara.) Nor should a funicular be confused with a cog railway, which generally accomplishes the same thing: it goes up and down impossibly steep terrain. The world's steepest cog railway climbs Mount Pilatus in Switzerland. The world's most boring one climbs Mount Washington in New Hampshire. Mount Washington, however, lays claim to having at its top the world's worst weather. A welcome diversion by the time you get there.

31

Q: Long before the invention of the mechanical clock, the Egyptians had a method of telling time, although they usually had to go outside to employ it. What was the device they used?

A: Of course, the sundial.

The Challenge

Q: How did they tell time at night?

A: **With "water clocks,"** similar in operation to sandglasses. The first mechanical timepiece on record (in China, in 1088) used water too, but for power, not monitoring. The first European clock was built at an English monastery in 1283. No water; it used weights. (Either way, it must have been a welcome replacement for the hot-foot alarm system commonly used in monasteries. In order that the rigid schedule of prayer laid down by Saint Benedict be kept, it was customary for one of the brothers to take on the role of alarm clock by sleeping with a lit candle between his toes.) The world's oldest clock in working order (1386) is on Salisbury Cathedral. The clock has no face, so you have to wait for the chime. Maybe not a good idea to wait under the tower, though. It's two feet off perpendicular at the top.

Mainsprings were developed in Germany around 1500, making watches possible, and right from the first they became a status symbol. Early ones were big and heavy, so wealthy owners usually had a servant tag along to carry theirs. Minute hands didn't appear until 1670. That too was in England, but it was in Geneva, in 1790, that the first wristwatch was made – *ten years after* the first self-winding watch (made in London in 1780 but not patented until 1924). The first waterproof watch (a Rolex) was made in 1926, and the first alarm watch was patented in France in 1947. Bulova didn't retail the quartz crystal watch until 1970, although it was developed in the 1920s.

In this flood of dates, 1945 deserves to be singled out. That's the year Big Ben lost five minutes because a huge murmuration of starlings perched on the minute hand, preventing it from moving.

32

Q: On April 28, 1789, six months out of Tahiti, part of the crew of HMS *Bounty*, led by Fletcher Christian, mutinied against Captain William Bligh. The mutineers put Bligh and those who remained loyal into a twenty-three-foot open boat, dumped the cargo overboard, and then turned the ship back toward Tahiti. Over time, the cargo, allegedly one of the causes of the mutiny because of the care it demanded, has become almost as well known as Bligh, Fletcher Christian, and the ship itself. What was the *Bounty* carrying?

A: Yes, breadfruit trees.

The Challenge

Q: Where was the *Bounty* going with the trees?

A: **To Jamaica.** In a way, the mutiny was another legacy of slavery. The *Bounty* was part of an experiment to grow bread-fruit in Jamaica as a cheap food staple for the slaves on sugar plantations. In 1791, Bligh repeated the Tahiti–Jamaica voyage, and this time delivered 300 live trees. They grew, but the exper-iment was a bust, for the slaves wouldn't eat breadfruit.

It's well known that the *Bounty* never saw England again. The famous *Mayflower* did, however. After delivering the Pilgrim Fathers (and mothers; there were 102 passengers when they left England and 103 when they landed, so . . .), she went back but was dismantled and turned into a barn! Hardly applaudable, but somewhat less embarrassing than the fate of the *Buccaneer*, a tug hired by the Royal Navy in 1947 to tow a gunnery target for the destroyer HMS *Saintes*. Apparently the *Saintes* really needed practice, for she sank the *Buccaneer* with her first salvo. The target drifted out to sea and, like the *Bounty*, was never seen again.

You could take bets that such a naval farce would never have occurred under Bligh's watch, for he was a captain of outstanding qualities. Unfortunately, one of those qualities was a profound lack of tolerance, and in 1808, as governor of New South Wales, he ran into another mutiny. There was no boat this time; the colonists put him in prison. Bligh was a survivor, though. After the *Bounty* mutiny, he'd made land in Indonesia in three months without charts or instruments. By 1814, he had become an admiral, which suggests that people skills ranked pretty low in the Royal Navy's criteria for pro-motion. Yet the man was not without admirers. An oft-ignored fact about the *Bounty* affair is that eighteen members of the crew remained loyal to him. Only seventeen had sided with Fletcher Christian.

33

Q: Although they were the first Olympics to be shown on television screens, the 1936 summer games in Berlin are best remembered for the upstaging of a Nazi propaganda program that taunted the United States for using inferior "black auxiliaries." Which American athlete upset this propaganda by winning four gold medals in track and field?

A: Right, Jesse Owens.

The Challenge

Q: Which nation topped the medal standings in the 1936 Olympics?

A Germany, with eighty-nine medals, against fifty-six for the second-place U.S.A.

The Germans athletes took the medals but the German people utterly lionized Owens, giving him the kind of recognition he couldn't seem to get at home. Only a year before, at the Big Ten Championships in Ann Arbor, Michigan, Jesse broke five world records and tied a sixth in the space of forty-five minutes, but the U.S. amateur athlete of the year award went to a golfer, Lawson Little. In 1936, the award went to single-gold-medal winner Glenn Morris. Also, it is not true that Hitler refused to congratulate Owens, but he *was* snubbed by President Roosevelt, who neither invited him to the White House nor sent him a letter of congratulations.

For Jesse Owens, a positive outcome of the 1936 Olympics was the development of a deep, but for the time and place improbable, friendship. German long jumper Luz Long was a tall, blue-eyed athlete, in appearance the model of Aryan superiority. During the long-jump trials, Owens got rattled and would likely have fouled out without Long's advice. When Owens beat Long a few hours later in the finals (Long got silver), the German athlete was first to congratulate him – with a big hug in front of the Nazi VIP seats. The two remained close friends until Long was killed in July 1943 at the Battle of St. Pietro. Owens passed away at age sixty-seven in 1980. He was a pack-a-day smoker for thirty-five years and died of lung cancer.

Among the many delicious footnotes to the 1936 games is the name of the silver medalist in the 200-meter event. "Mack" Robinson finished four-tenths of a second behind Jesse Owens. Eleven years later, Mack's kid brother Jackie made history in major league baseball.

34

Q: Most animals have two levels of response when they're threatened. The first level is a "Back off!" warning. Dogs bark, cats hiss, lions roar, and silverback gorillas thump their chests. At the second level of response, they either turn and run or else they attack. Now, this should be well known: At the second level, what do skunks do?

A: Indeed, they spray.

The Challenge

Q: What is a skunk's first-level response?

A: **It faces the aggressor, thumps its paws on the ground, and lifts its tail.** (Don't count on all three actions every time. Skunks are not I.Q. leaders in the animal world.)

In the interest of olfactory comfort, here are some skunk facts that are best to acquire academically rather than through personal experience. At the second level, a skunk will point its tail in the direction of the aggressor and spray. That means no matter where you happen to be standing, front, back, or either side, you're going to get it. The range for the spray is up to twelve feet (four meters), but humans can pick up skunk smell two miles (three kilometers) away! We're not sure how helpful this is, but skunk spray is a sulphide called mercaptan, and the active chemical is ethanethiol. Should you have opportunity to elevate the discussion at your next board meeting with this information, you might wish to add that one part of ethanethiol per ten trillion is detectable by the average human nose under laboratory conditions.

For filing under "gross-out": The spray is an oily, greenish fluid produced in a pair of musk sacs and discharged through the anus. (If you're wondering just who spends time figuring out this stuff, you might reflect on Hennig Brand, who discovered phosphorous in 1669 while analyzing urine.)

Finally, skunks are omnivorous. They eat grubs, beetles, mice, fruits, and vegetables, and, like raccoons, have discovered that urban environments suit their lifestyle eminently well. Eggs have an almost overwhelming appeal for them. Biologists calculate that raising chickens increases your chances of attracting a skunk by several hundred percent, so keep your leghorns off the balcony.

35

Q: Red tunics and well-groomed black horses, both of which have been strictly ceremonial for decades, have made this police force the most recognizable gendarmerie in the world. What is its name?

A: Yes, the RCMP, the Royal Canadian Mounted Police – the Mounties – or, as insiders call it, "the Force."

The Challenge

Q: What is the well-known motto of the Mounties?

A: *"Maintiens le droit"* ("Uphold the right" in English), *not* "They get their man." The popular – and incorrect – phrase is usually attributed to Hollywood, but it first appeared in 1877, two years after the official motto was adopted.

Interestingly, many Canadians think that *"Maintiens le droit"* translates as "Maintain the right," an ironic touch given that the Mounties are in charge of traffic control in all but two of Canada's provinces. Even more ironic if you reflect on the role of right- versus left-handedness in some types of crime. Left-handers make up about 10% of the human population, yet they are significantly over-represented among sexual psychopaths. The elusive Jack the Ripper, it is known, was left-handed. Likewise Albert DeSalvo, a.k.a. the Boston Strangler. Left-handers also have more than average trouble playing saxophones; knitting is often a problem; and what must be truly distressing: since 1909, no sinistromanual has ever won the world horseshoe-pitching championship.

Still, the news is not all bad. Left-handers find it easier to unscrew jar-tops and to write most Semitic scripts. They are also over-represented among geniuses. Nicola Tesla was a leftie; so was Benjamin Franklin. Also, certain lefties seem to be far more co-ordinated and finely tuned than the rest of the world. Babe Ruth, for example, could read the label of a 78-rpm record while it was spinning. On the other hand (no pun intended), President Gerald Ford was left-handed.

Parents who plan ahead take note: A study at the University of Manchester in 1981 concluded that a first-time mother's chances of giving birth to a leftie increase as she ages. At age thirty-nine, the possibility is 43%. There are no data on the chances of giving birth to a potential Mountie.

36

Q: For an extended period beginning in 1960, motel owners noticed a significant drop in the use of showers by their guests, a phenomenon attributed to Anthony Perkins's scary attack on Janet Leigh in Alfred Hitchcock's movie *Psycho*. What is the name of Perkins's character in this movie?

A: Right, Norman Bates. Norman murders Janet Leigh's character in the shower at the Bates Motel.

The Challenge

Q: What is the name of Janet Leigh's character?

A: **Marion Crane.** So you don't have to look it up, Vera Miles played Lila Crane, Martin Balsam, who also died scarily, was Milton Arbogast, John Gavin was Sam Loomis, and Simon Oakland was Dr. Rickman. John McIntire was the no-name sheriff.

Moviegoers who love thrillers but are fed up with violence pray daily for another Alfred Hitchcock, or at least a rebirth of his talent for making an audience gasp without resorting to shlock-shock. Marion's death is one of the most frightening murders in film history. She's a woman at her most vulnerable, naked in the shower, attacked by a madman. Yet not once is Norman's very long and threatening knife ever seen to actually touch her body. Even the blood – very little of it by contemporary standards of gore – was ordinary, innocent chocolate syrup! (Worked nicely in a black-and-white movie.) The look of shock on Marion's face is genuine, however. Without warning Leigh it was going to happen, Hitchcock arranged that at the crucial moment, the water in the shower suddenly become ice-cold. (Another authentic facial expression in the movies is the one of pain on Gary Cooper's face in *High Noon* (1952). Just before filming, Cooper was hospitalized for a hernia. During filming he had a hip injury. After filming he had surgery for a duodenal ulcer.)

The name Bates comes up again in the film version of Stephen King's spooky novel *Carrie*. Bates High School was Carrie's alma mater. In real life the Bateses fare somewhat better. Harry Bates (1850–99) achieved fame as a sculptor. Henry Bates (1825–92) recorded over 8,000 new species of insects. Daisy Bates (1860–1951) was one of Australia's first social workers. Still, if you ever stay at a Bates Motel, you may want to avoid Unit 1. That was Marion Crane's room.

Q: Who was the founder of Scouting, or Boy Scouts, as it was first known?

A: Yes, Robert Baden-Powell, or if you want the whole thing, Lieutenant-General (ret.) Robert Stephenson Smyth Baden-Powell, First Baron Gilwell, KCVO, KCB, OM. His wife's name was Lady Olave St. Clair Baden-Powell. (They sent very large Christmas cards.)

The Challenge

Q: Who was the founder of Girl Scouts (a.k.a. Girl Guides)?

A: **Baden-Powell**, with his sister Agnes. The Boy Scouts were started in 1907, the Girl Scouts in 1910.

Most Scouts never learn how B.-P. tried out the many outdoor and survival skills the Scouting movement teaches, the ones in his book, *Aids for Scouting*. Robert Baden-Powell was, in effect, a spy for the British army. (He was also a general, but that was later.) Whether or not spying fits the ethical image that Scouting projects, B.-P. was, by all accounts, most effective in the role. By pretending to be a nutcase butterfly collector, he was able to run about freely, net in hand, on the grounds of military forts throughout Germany, France, Tunisia, and Algeria. After a thorough reconnaissance, he would sit down and, under the very noses of the bemused sentries, make sketches of captive lepidoptera – along with a particular fort's layout, gun size and placement, and any other information of value. That was in the 1880s and 1890s. After that, B.-P. did a tour of South Africa in the guise of a correspondent. What he was really there for was to check the accuracy of British military maps. When the Boer War began, he had a more hands-on military role, and achieved fame in the siege at Mafeking in 1900, holding out for 215 days until relieved.

Neither last nor least on the scale of B.-P.'s gifts to the world is a delightful addition to the English lexicon. The hollow necktie-knot substitute that snugs a neckerchief at the throat on a Scout's uniform is called a woggle. The cord that goes around the neckerchief and down the chest is a lanyard – not at all as impressive a word as woggle. (Besides, lanyards are also used to fire cannon. Can't do that with a woggle.)

Q: In the same year that he is credited with breaking the color barrier in major league baseball, Jackie Robinson won the National League Rookie of the Year Award. What year was that?

A: Yes, 1947.

The Challenge

Q: The next year, 1948, the American League offered its Rookie of the Year Award to a black player. He turned it down. With real class, too. Who was this player?

A. **Leroy "Satchel" Paige.** In 1948, Paige was forty-two years old, with a hugely successful career in the Negro Leagues already behind him. His explanation of the refusal is a gem: "[I] didn't know which year those gentlemen had in mind." When he began his pro career in 1926 with the Birmingham Black Barons, "Satchel" had been training by throwing strikes over a bottle cap. When he retired from the Kansas City Athletics in 1965, he was fifty-nine and still pitching.

Major league baseball has still not come to grips with accomplishments in the Negro Baseball Leagues. Despite technical arguments, mostly about the "officialness" of stats, the reality is that Negro League teams were professional, and they enlisted some astonishingly powerful players. Think of the great Josh Gibson and his 75 home runs in one season. Or pitcher Dick "Cannonball" Redding: 25 strikeouts in one game and 30 career no-hitters. Another pitcher, Wilbur Rogan, was a career 113–45 with the Kansas City Monarchs, and never batted under .300! Another eyebrow-raiser: Of the documented exhibition games against white major league teams, the Negro Leagues won over 60%.

Recognizing the Negro Leagues would definitely stir up a hornet's nest. To begin with, Jackie Robinson would likely have to be retroactively disqualified for his 1947 award, because he played professionally in 1945 (Kansas City Monarchs). Really, he wasn't even the "famous first." In 1884, an African American, Moses Fleetwood Walker, caught 42 games (bare-handed) for the Toledo Blue Stockings of the American Association, a professional team in a professional league. Walker was college-educated and a pioneer in racial integration. He played in four different leagues before being barred for his color in 1890.

Q: In *A Christmas Carol*, the Dickens character Bob Cratchit is called a "clerk." For someone who records debits and credits, as Bob did, we would be more likely, today, to use a different professional label. It's one of only two words in English that have three double letters in a row. What is the word?

A: Of course, bookkeeper.

The Challenge

Q: What other English word has three double letters in a row?

A: **Tattooee.** Words like this stir the souls of language pedants, so before they tell you, tell *them* that there is only one single-syllable English word with four consecutive vowels: queue. If they nod knowingly (almost for sure), add the fact that facetious and abstemious are the only words with all five vowels used once and in alphabetical order, that the only word with three dots in a row is hijinks, that strengths has nine letters but only one vowel, and that indivisibility has but one vowel, used six times! (The letter Y is not a vowel, so if you're up against a super-pedant, say ". . . uses only one of the five vowels . . ." when you pose this particular insight.) We acknowledge that you may find the odd shoddy dictionary that fails to list tattooee. A strange omission, for just as mortgagors need mortgagees and lessors need lessees, tattooers need – well, you get the idea.

Tattoo, like atoll, is one of only a handful of English words to come from Polynesian. Curiously, the most tattooed male in the world lives nowhere near the Pacific. He's Tom Leopard of the Isle of Skye. Also very far from the etymological source is the world's most tattooed female, Krystyne Kolorful. She's a dancer from Alberta. Judging by a study in the *American Journal of Psychiatry*, both Tom and Krystyne would have been one and a half times more likely to be rejected for service in the U.S. armed forces in World War II. The study says that during the war, "neuro-psychiatric abnormality" was the stated reason for rejecting 58% of tattooees. (See! There's the word in use.)

40

Q: Where is the world's largest basilica?

A: Yes, in Rome. The Basilica of St. Peter is about five and a half acres (2.2 hectares) in area.

The Challenge

Q: Where is the world's tallest basilica?

A: **In Yamoussoukro, Ivory Coast.** It's the Basilica of Our Lady of Peace. You get points if you actually knew there is a basilica there, and a bonus if you can spell Yamoussoukro on the first try. If you're making notes, the world's largest synagogue, Temple Emanu-El in New York, is just under an acre (0.4 hectares), and the world's largest mosque, the Shah Faisal Mosque in Islamabad, is about 1.2 acres (0.5 hectares).

Of all these famous buildings, only St. Peter's has experienced an unauthorized climb on the outside by a tourist. In the winter of 1817, English adventurer Charles Waterton climbed the dome, then the cross, and hung his gloves on the lightning rod. Pope Pius VII was not amused, especially when not a single Roman would go up to get the gloves, so Waterton graciously returned and scrambled up a second time.

Whether Waterton was courageous or crazy is a moot point. Over his three excursions to the Amazon, Waterton contributed very significantly to the emerging sciences of zoology and taxidermy, but his methods were, to say the least, unorthodox. Here is his 1809 journal entry on the capture of a ten-foot anaconda:

"The snake came on at me . . . hissing and open-mouthed, within two feet of my face, and then, with all the force I was master of, I drove my fist, shielded by my hat, full in his jaws . . . He was stunned. I seized him round the throat with both hands . . . and allowed him to coil round my body. He pressed me hard but not alarmingly so."

Another entry describes his discovery that one man can hold an alligator's jaws closed while astride its back. This enlightenment came at about the time he was keeping an uncaged sloth in his room.

Waterton died peacefully in his bed in England.

41

Q: The date: October 26, 1881. The city: Tombstone, Arizona. The event: a gunfight. On one side, outlaws Ike and Billy Clanton, along with their neighbors Tom and Frank McLaury; on the other, a consumptive, off-and-on dentist, John "Doc" Halliday, and three brothers. Who were these brothers?

A: Of course, the Earps, Virgil, Morgan, and Wyatt.

The Challenge

Q: Where did this legendary gunfight take place?

A: No, not at the OK Corral, but on a vacant lot between Camillus Fly's Rooming House and Photographic Studio and the private home of lumber dealer W. A. Harwood. The OK Corral was about forty giant steps to the east.

Either killing was no big deal in Tombstone or the editor of the Tombstone *Epitaph* had other priorities on his mind, for the event only made it onto page 3 of the next edition. Racy headline, though: "Three Men Hurled Into Eternity In The Duration Of A Moment." The McLaurys and Billy Clanton made up the three. Despite damaging testimony against the Earps – witnesses said they had fired without cause – they and Halliday were exonerated.

It was author Stuart Lake who, in his 1931 biography, *Wyatt Earp: Frontier Marshal*, moved the fight to the corral. The city of Tombstone, to support the legend and attract tourists, then enlarged the corral to encompass the spot where the fight actually occurred. This bit of clever marketing lagged behind the efforts of Zeralda James by some years, however. The mother of Frank and Jesse, shortly after the latter's death in 1882, set up a shrine at her son's grave in Missouri. Tourists, if they brought enough cash, could buy one of the rocks that covered the gravesite.

The sign for OK, a circle of thumb and forefinger, originated with the Roman rhetorician Quintilian, not with semi-literate President Andrew Jackson, who supposedly approved documents with "Orl Keerect," nor with Martin Van Buren, who was from Old Kinderhook, NY. Quintilian used the gesture in his oratory classes to signify approval. Be circumspect in your use of it. In many parts of Europe, the thumb-and-forefinger circle is seen as a very rude gesture.

Q: When a fertile seed lies on a shelf, it just, well, lies there. But when it is planted in the ground, it grows roots that go down and shoots that grow up. Once this happens, the seed is said to have . . . To have what?

A: Yes, germinated.

The Challenge

Q: How does the seed know to send the roots down and shoots up, and not the other way round?

A: **Gravity.** The seed contains an embryo in which certain hormones sense the ups and downs of gravitational pull and, without even thinking about Isaac Newton, react accordingly. The process is called gravitropism, a term that, unfortunately, gets about as much use as campanography (the art of bell-ringing) or onyxectomy (de-clawing).

It is true that a falling apple inspired Newton to develop his laws of gravity, but the thing didn't actually hit him on the head. He saw one fall at just the moment when he was thinking about the idea. Newton didn't really need a cranial insult anyway. Like many geniuses, he was weird enough to begin with. This legendary school dropout (urged by his mother to quit and become a farmer; he wasn't doing very well anyway), one of the inventors of calculus, the discoverer of the spectral composition of light, the fundamentals of optics, and the basic laws of mechanics — all before his mid-twenties — felt personally that his greatest work was an interpretation of the Book of Daniel. His manuscript on the subject, written with a quill, runs to several million words.

Newton's biblical effort is somewhat more extensive than his contribution to the British House of Commons, where he was an MP for two terms. The precisely kept records of that august institution reveal that over that time, his only utterance was a request to open a window.

◁ **43** ▷

Q: On August 3, 1968, a system known as the Direct Communications link was set up between Washington, D.C., and Moscow. By what name is this telephone line popularly known?

A: Of course, the "hot line." It was set up to enable emergency consultation so that accidental nuclear war might be avoided.

The Challenge

Q: Was the hot line ever used?

A: Yes. The first time was in 1967, during the Arab-Israeli war of that year. The communication between Lyndon Johnson's office and Nikolai Podgorny's was essentially of the we-won't-if-you-won't variety, since neither superpower was keen to have that war continue.

The Washington–Moscow hot line has had a somewhat smoother history than the red telephone link between Washington and Ottawa, set up in 1958 as part of NORAD, a nuclear defense pact between the U.S. and Canada. President Eisenhower kept his red telephone in a desk drawer in the Oval Office, but after Jackie Kennedy renovated in 1961, no one could find the phone. She got rid of the desk, along with much of the furniture in the White House, and the phone was disconnected and thrown out!

At the Canadian end, the red phone had two levels of exposure in the early days. Prime Minister John Diefenbaker kept it front and center on his desk ("I can call Ike anytime" was a favorite claim) but his successor, Prime Minister Lester Pearson, was far less interested in image (or organization) and gradually allowed the red phone to disappear under mounds of paper. Until it rang one winter morning in 1964. After a mad scramble to find it, Pearson finally picked up and heard a voice say, "Is Charlie there?" By a twist of technology that has never been satisfactorily explained to security forces in either Canada or the U.S., a caller had dialed a wrong number and got through on one of the world's most private lines.

◁ **44** ▷

Q: According to the record of history, who was first to cross the Americas from Atlantic to Pacific?

A: Right, Balboa, Vasco Núñez de Balboa. He crossed modern-day Panama in 1513. Although members of the native population must certainly have done it long before he did, Balboa is the first on record.

The Challenge

Q: Who was first to go *around* the Americas?

A: The scientists and crew aboard the CSS *Hudson*, a Canadian government research vessel, from November 1969 to November 1970. The *Hudson* sailed south from Halifax, Nova Scotia, around Cape Horn, north to the Bering Sea, through the Northwest Passage, and back to Halifax. Along the way, they did an in-depth study of the fjords of Chile, which may be one reason why there's never been a movie made about this trip.

Nor has the accomplishment ever been acknowledged in poetry, unlike that of Balboa. English Romantic poet John Keats immortalized Balboa by calling him "stout Cortez," which suggests that both Keats and his editor were graduates of the same kind of curriculum that credits the first crossing of the Americas to Meriwether Lewis and William Clark in 1804–06. Although their journey was longer, these two lagged Balboa by about 300 years. Not only that, they made their trek more than a decade *after* explorer and fur trader Alexander Mackenzie crossed Canada on a trip that was longer yet. Mackenzie crossed in stages from Halifax to Montreal, then on to Lake Athabasca, and from there to the Arctic and the Pacific. He then wrote a book about his adventures: *Voyages from Montreal Through the Continent of North America.* Thomas Jefferson read it, was intrigued by the idea, and turned to his private secretary, Meriwether Lewis . . .

None of these explorers would likely have succeeded without the help of the indigenous peoples. Lewis and Clark accomplished this peacefully for the most part, although they did get into skirmishes. Balboa went out of his way to slaughter. He even used a pack of attack dogs on his journey. Only Mackenzie was able to make the claim that not one shot was fired in anger.

Q: A "road" in the Far East that was made famous well before Bob Hope, Bing Crosby, and Dorothy Lamour began making movies is this one in Burma. A poem by Rudyard Kipling gets the credit. It even became a popular song. It's the road to . . . where?

A: Of course, the road to Mandalay.

The Challenge

Q: To Mandalay from where?

A: **Rangoon.** It's actually not a road but the Irrawaddy River in Burma (today the Republic of Myanmar) which Kipling was celebrating, a difference which makes couplets like "On the road to Mandalay, / Where the flyin'-fishes play," somewhat more defensible. Whether or not Kipling ever paddled all the way from Rangoon to Mandalay is moot. If indeed he did, then judging by lines like "An' the dawn comes up like thunder outer China 'crost the Bay!" he must have slept in every day, for there's no bay east of the Irrawaddy for the sun to rise over. There's only Thailand. But then, a line like ". . . thunder outer China 'crost Thailand," although it's better geography, would have made for lousy rhyme. (Of course, he'd have said "Siam.")

The editor of the San Francisco *Examiner*, who once fired Kipling, didn't have a problem with the writer's geography, and clearly was not impressed by his facility with rhyme. According to the pink slip, Kipling "just doesn't know how to use the English language." Given that shortly after, Kipling won the 1907 Nobel Prize for Literature, he must have made significant remedial strides in a very short time.

Apart from winning this prize, producing a huge canon of very popular writing, and inventing snow golf (played with red balls), Kipling distinguished himself by giving the original manuscript for *The Jungle Book* to the nurse of his first child, telling her she might use it some day if she ever needed money. After he died, she was able to live in comfort on the proceeds.

46

Q: An article of faith among undergraduates during that period of doubt between the end of term and the publishing of final grades is that marks are invariably adjusted by distributing them along a mathematical curve. What is this curve called?

A: Indeed, a bell curve.

The Challenge

Q: "Bell curve" is a street name. What is this distribution more properly called?

A: **A Gaussian curve**, or sometimes Gaussian distribution (also known as a normal curve/distribution, due to its widespread appearance in nature). It's named after Karl Friedrich Gauss (1777–1855), who was in his teens when he proposed it. A true genius and math whiz, Gauss is also responsible for items like the following quick-add formula. (He figured this one out at age twelve.) To add up all the numbers between, say, 1 and 200 – this assumes you would want to – instead of slogging through $1 + 2 + 3 + 4 \ldots$, multiply the end number (200) by the middle one (100) and then add the middle number: $200 \times 100 + 100 = 20,100$. It works every time, and it's fast. Try again. The sum of the numbers between, say, 1 and 36 is $36 \times 18 + 18 = 666$.

If the end number is odd, e.g., 37, you multiply it by one half of the next lowest even number ($36 \times 1/2 = 18$) and then add the end number. Don't quit; it's easy! $37 \times 18 + 37 = 703$. Not hard to see why many of Gauss's ideas have had a major impact on the world. Yet even he didn't bat 1.000. One of his ideas, planting ten-mile (sixteen-kilometer) strips of trees in Siberia in the shape of the Pythagorean theorem to demonstrate to extraterrestrials that earthlings know geometry, has never been taken up with any enthusiasm.

As marriage partners, geniuses are often high-risk prospects. Gauss was no exception. One day in 1807, while he was in his study working on yet another mathematical insight, his wife lay dying upstairs. At the crucial moment their family physician knocked on the study door.

"Herr Gauss, her time has come," the doctor said.

"Tell her to wait a moment until I'm through," Gauss replied.

47

Q: It's not a phrase that Sister Angelica would have approved of after a hockey game (or at any other time), but "sweat like a horse" is often heard in the dressing room. Do horses sweat?

A: Sure, along with many other animals. Apes are particularly bad. Cows sweat; so do sheep — and why not, under all that blanket? Even hippopotami sweat (the sweat's red, incidentally).

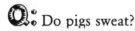

The Challenge

Q: Do pigs sweat?

A: No. They are very susceptible to sunburn too, but the reason they so often wallow in mud has more to do with lack of perspiration than lack of sunblock. Wallowing keeps them cool, but gives them some very bad press. "Dirty as a pig" is one outcome. "Lazy as a pig" is another. Only one of these epithets actually comes close to the truth.

Under appropriate conditions, pigs will keep themselves clean. In a pen, for instance, they are ever careful to go potty in a chosen area, well away from where they feed and sleep. Because it's a group-monitored behavior, and because pigs, like all animals, have slow learners in their midst, it's quite common to see them body-blocking one of their own over to the chosen area if they see him or her about to commit a social disgrace. Unfortunately, pigs are very much victims of their internal thermodynamics, and are almost living proof that too much heat can scramble your brains. Once the ambient temperature goes above 84°F (29°C), they seem to lose all sense of intelligent behavior, and as for targeted defecation, well, the floor's the limit.

Humans, who, like pigs, are one of the very few species to make conscious decisions about where to perform bodily functions, are at the top of the heap when it comes to mammal sweat, with men exuding at double the rate of women (except during menopausal and postpartum flashes). Camels are like pigs in that they hardly sweat at all, but the similarity ends there. If you ever hike along a caravan route, be sure to watch where you put your feet.

48

Q: Quite likely, your mother quoted this proverb to you at some point in your childhood. You may say it now yourself. It's widely known, and even atheists and agnostics have been heard to use it. It goes: "Cleanliness is next to . . ." Next to what?

A: Right, godliness.

The Challenge

Q: Where did this proverb originate?

A: In **"Sermon 93: On Dress"** by John Wesley (1703–91), founder of the Methodist Church. It's not from the Bible.

To be entirely accurate, it's really only the memorable wording that should be credited to Wesley, for he lifted the idea from Hebrew sage Phinehas ben-Yair. (Unfortunately, no one ever bothers to look carefully at "Sermon 93," where Wesley has quotation marks around the famous phrase, presumably an acknowledgment that it came from elsewhere.)

It's not hard to attribute stuff to Wesley, for as a writer he produced at industrial levels, churning out hymns, sermons, journals, grammars, histories, biographies, translations from Greek, Latin, and Hebrew, a dictionary, and, one of his more remarkable works, a home-cure advisory piece on medicine entitled *Primitive Physic*. This treatise offers recommendations such as the following: "For hoarseness: rub the soles of the feet with garlic and lard." "For toothache: a leaf of betony (lousewort) put up the nose."

Much of what Wesley wrote on matters of religion and morals was off-putting to his contemporaries. However, his medical advice was very favorably received, perhaps owing to counsel like this: "For consumption: every morning cut a small turf of fresh earth and, lying down, breathe into the hole for fifteen minutes. In the last stages, suck a healthy woman daily." For doubters on this one, he adds, "This cured my father."

In "Sermon 93," written about the same time as *Primitive Physic*, Wesley admonishes his congregation to revere cleanliness. But the medical book does not reveal how Wesley's father, Samuel, resolved the issue of staying clean while lying down on the "small turf of fresh earth," unless perhaps he skipped this part and went straight to "the last stages." Since John was Samuel's fifteenth child, that's a plausible bit of speculation.

49

Q: If you settled into your easy chair on a weekend afternoon to watch "the Masters," what sport would you be watching?

A: Of course, golf. This annual tournament, called "the U.S. Masters" outside North America, was first held in 1934.

The Challenge

Q: If you were watching "the Benson & Hedges Masters," what sport would you be watching?

A. **Snooker.** The payout for winners of the golfing Masters is somewhat higher than the prize money for the Benson & Hedges Masters, but then, snooker players don't have to tip caddies or rent carts, and they can keep on playing even if a thunderstorm blows up. Not that snooker champions are on the dole. Canadian Cliff Thorburn, for example, who has won the B&H Masters twice (so far the only non-Brit to do so), was retained by the sultan of Brunei to teach snooker to his son at $3,000 an hour.

Unlike golf, which is by far the world's most land-consuming game — Mark Twain said it spoils a good walk — snooker requires only a twelve by six and a half foot (3.66 m x 1.98 m) table and a room big enough to house it. Conveniently, that is also the official size of an English billiards table, and there was one of those in the officers' mess at Jubbulpore, India, when Neville Chamberlain arrived in 1875 as a subaltern with the Devonshire Regiment. At the time, the big game in the mess was "black pool," and it was this game that Chamberlain modified and called "snooker," a sobriquet applied to new cadets at the Royal Military Institute at Sandhurst. In 1882, the game was shown to British pool pro John Roberts at the Ootacamund Club in Calcutta, and it was he who took it home and spread it throughout England. (Roberts was in Calcutta to tutor the maharajah of Cooch Behar in billiards. Obviously, there's an industry here.)

Snooker settled easily and quickly into Europe, where billiards had long been popular. The imprisoned Mary Queen of Scots complained, in 1576, that not only were her quarters too cold and too close to the loo, but that her billiard table had been removed.

50

Q: Except for Anne Boleyn, wife number two of Henry VIII, the mates of this famous king are not very well known. Even so, you can probably come up with the total number quickly enough. How many wives did Henry VIII have?

A: Yes, indeed, six. An easy way to remember them: three Catherines, two Annes, and a Jane.

The Challenge

Q: How many children did Henry have?

A: **Three.** Mary I with Catherine of Aragon (wife number one), Elizabeth I with Boleyn, and Edward VI with Jane Seymour (number three).

Granted, the true total is probably murky here. Randy royals abound in history, and Henry sure didn't get his case of syphilis from a toilet seat, although there was a determined effort to spread the word that he got it from Cardinal Wolsey always whispering in his ear. Nor was the atmosphere of the court at all discouraging in matters of promiscuity. Case in point: A ruling passed by Henry's officer of the bedchamber decreed that "Such pages as cause maids of the King's household to become mothers shall go without beer for a month." Modern-day visitors to the Tower of London, where Henry's personal armor is on display, would surely not attribute his failure to produce a string of male heirs to any anatomical shortcomings on his part. The size of the protective codpiece that graces this particular suit is jaw-dropping. Whether it is a legitimate facsimile of the real thing or just an astute compliment from the royal armor makers, it definitely implies that in Henry's court, a high level of importance was attached to reproduction.

Quite possibly, the court of his time might have benefitted from more role models like the wife of the Duke of York, second son of George III. She never went to bed, but lay fully dressed on a couch all night, surrounded by troops of dogs, monkeys, and parrots — never less than forty — while a lady-in-waiting read to her. She never had any children, legitimate or otherwise.

51

Q: Audiences guffawed at the opening scenes of Elvis Presley's first movie, a post–Civil War effort in which the sight of the King in overalls, behind a plough, was not what they expected. But the giggles faded when Elvis sang the movie's signature song. It had the same title as the movie and became a huge hit, sung long after the movie was mercifully forgotten. What is this soft ballad, so opposite in style to hits like "Hound Dog," "Don't Be Cruel," and "Jailhouse Rock"?

A: Right, "Love Me Tender." The lyrics are credited to Presley and Vera Matson, but the melody is a straight lift from a song written in 1861, itself a big hit throughout the Civil War.

The Challenge

Q: What song did Presley and Matson reword?

A: **"Aura Lee"**; words by W. W. Fosdick, music by G. R. Poulton. Their song begins, "As the blackbird in the spring, 'neath the willow tree . . . ," whereas the modern one starts, "Love me tender, love me sweet, never let me go." "Aura Lee" is often wrongly credited to Stephen Foster.

Whether or not Dr. Legrand G. Capers, a Civil War surgeon in Mississippi, was anticipating Presley's lyrics, we can't be sure, but in an 1874 issue of *The American Medical Weekly*, he reported treating a young Confederate soldier for injuries caused by a stray minié ball that passed through his reproductive organs during the Battle of Raymond. In itself, not an event worthy of publication, but the bullet, after its first adventure, then penetrated a young lady standing on her porch nearby. She became pregnant and, understandably bewildered, presented herself to Dr. Capers, who then put two and two together, so to speak. The sperm-carrying bullet is on display today at the Old Courthouse Museum in Vicksburg, MS, along with an insistent testimonial from Dr. Capers that the phenomenon really did occur.

For readers who feel inclined to dispute the possible provenance of projectile-borne sperm, here is a piece of modern research into the mating practices of *Drosophila bifurca* (giant fruit fly) that deserves some thought. The male of this species delivers sperm via what is called the peashooter effect: it actually fires sperm pellets through the air by means of what, for lack of a better term, is called by scientists his peashooter. Researchers have yet to demonstrate, however, whether the male fruit fly's accuracy is enhanced by a soft rendering of "Love Me Tender."

52

Q: All the women most closely involved with Napoleon Bonaparte were named Maria. There was Maria Letizia, Maria Louisa, Maria Anna Elisa, Maria Joséphine, Maria Paulina, and Maria Annunciata. Which Maria was Napoleon's first, and best-known, wife?

A: Of course, Joséphine (Maria Joséphine Rose), six years his senior and widow of the guillotined Alexandre de Beauharnais who fought in the American Revolution. The second wife was Maria Louisa.

The Challenge

Q: Which Maria was Napoleon's mother?

A: **The first one, Maria Letizia** (*née* Ramolino). No surprise that she was a woman of powerful will, not to mention constitution. Maria Letizia outlived her husband by fifty-one years and her famous son by fifteen.

Despite Letizia's considerable influence on Napoleon's personal habits, she does not seem to have instilled in him the idea of a daily bath. In fact there's reason to believe that the Emperor much preferred the *au naturel* style. In a letter to Joséphine from Italy in 1800, Napoleon initiated foreplay this way: "Home in three days. Don't wash!"

Not that Letizia's omission in the hygiene department necessarily merits criticism. It wasn't until the twentieth century that the idea of regular bathing really caught on. For those who yearn for the good old days, a letter from Michelangelo's father to his son, newly departed for Rome, is remarkably instructive. "Stay away from the baths," the older man warned, "but scrape yourself from time to time."

Whether they bathed or not, the Marias all did well by Napoleon. Sister Anna Elisa became a princess and a grand duchess, Paulina a duchess, and Annunciata a queen. Wife number two, Louisa, who fulfilled her sole purpose in the grand design by producing Napoleon II, stayed royal after her husband's demise, but she had been a royal to begin with, the daughter of Francis I of Austria. (One of the few conditions she imposed on the Emperor before moving in was that all paintings of Austrian defeats be removed from their several residences.)

Curiously (or perhaps not), only Mom never got a big position.

Being named Maria was common practice at the time. Victor Maria Hugo, Karl Maria von Weber, Maria Anna Mozart, and José María de Heredia are just a few examples.

Q: Of all the records in major league baseball, a sport obsessed with statistics, one continues to rest atop the pile. In 1961, Roger Eugene Maris of the New York Yankees hit 61 home runs, finally breaking the record for most home runs in a single season, set in 1927 by this player, also a New York Yankee. The player?

A: Of course, Babe Ruth.

The Challenge

Q: Whose record did Ruth break in 1927?

A: His own. He hit 59 homers in 1921, breaking the record held until then by Roger Connor, who played in the National League from 1880 to 1896. Since Connor's career home run total is 137, one of those seventeen years had to be a big one. All these stats, of course, ignore the records set by Josh Gibson, who hit 75 dingers in 1934 while playing in the Negro Leagues. On the other hand, no other great hitter has ever matched Babe Ruth's pitching prowess. For example, from 1917 until 1960, when he was done one better by Whitey Ford, Ruth held the World Series record for consecutive score-less innings pitched (29 2/3).

George Herman Ruth was being trained as a tailor at St. Mary's Industrial School in Baltimore when he was discovered by a big league scout. By Ruth's own account, he would have been a lousy tailor, and judging by a comment he made to President Harding at a Washington Senators–Yankees game in 1922 ("Hot as hell, ain't it, Prez?"), he'd have been even worse as a diplomat.

This rather pronounced lack of restraint had shown up before in Ruth's career. On June 23, 1917, while on the mound for the Boston Red Sox, he walked the first batter on four pitches. His response was to punch out umpire "Brick" Owens, for which, naturally, Ruth was ejected. Pitcher Ernie Shore then came in to throw the only perfect game ever thrown, thus far, by a reliever.

As for Roger Maris, other than his 1961 feat, he owns remarkably little space in the annals of baseball trivia, except for the fact that for years, the *Guinness Book of Records* listed him in the wrong league.

54

Q: Radio stations regularly give listeners a time signal, usually on the hour, and always at noon and midnight. What is the signal they give?

A: Right, a beep, or, if you prefer, a beeping sound. (If you're looking to embellish an upcoming episode of luncheon chit-chat, the technical name for this beep is "time mark" or "time pip"; insiders usually say just "pip." The length of the pip may vary by several nanoseconds from station to station.)

The Challenge

Q: Does the hour start at the beginning or the end of the pip?

A: **At the beginning.** For a world utterly obsessed with precise time, these pips have huge importance. Their use is controlled by the *Bureau International de l'Heure*, which has also given us the leap second, the first such arbitrary time adjustment since Pope Gregory fiddled with the Julian calendar in 1582. As necessary, a leap second is inserted or taken out at the end of March, June, September, or December to account for differences between International Atomic Time (precise to the nth power) and the earth's yearly rotation period, which normally is 31,556,925.9747 seconds but may be out by up to three seconds because the planet's axis has a tendency to wobble. What this means is that radio stations in places as widely diverse as Upper Dildo, Newfoundland, and Yogyakarta, Indonesia, can always get their pips straight, a remarkable achievement given that just over a hundred years ago, most communities were setting their clocks to 12 noon, when the sun was at its zenith overhead. Thus, until Canadian scientist Sandford Fleming convinced the world to standardize, when it was noon in Cincinnati, it was 12:04 in Toledo and 12:11 in Cleveland.

If you happen to be in England on a spring morning, you might opt for tuning in to birdsongs rather than time pips to set your watch. Ornithologists there agree that the following sequence is both correct and reliable. The greenfinch begins singing at 1:30 a.m., the blackcap an hour later, and the quail begins whistling at 3. At 4, the blackbirds check in, and a half hour later come the robins, wrens, and thrushes. Larks, sparrows, tomtits, and great tits are the last to get going, about 5 a.m., but by that time you should be up anyway.

55

Q: Any trivia buff can tell you that Marilyn Monroe was a Playmate of the Month. The same buff will be quick to tell you about another movie star who once posed — fully dressed — for the 1940 Montgomery Ward catalogue. That star?

A: Right, Gregory Peck.

The Challenge

Q: Even a non-buff can tell you that Marilyn Monroe's mother called her daughter Norma Jean. What did Mrs. Peck call her little boy?

A: Eldred. He was born Eldred Peck. The switch to Gregory is a reasonably modest one for Hollywood; somewhat less radical, for example, than that by Larry Rivers, who was born Yitroch Loiza Grossberg. Or Bobby Darin, born Walden Robert Cassotto, or Pola Negri, born Apolonia Mathias Chalupec. And a great deal less radical than Maria Rosario Pilar Martinez Melina Baeza and Cherilyn Sarkasian LaPierre, who became Charo and Cher respectively. Still another salute to simplicity is Ann-Margret, who began as Ann-Margaret Olsen (no relation, incidentally, to Harry Olsen, inventor of the electronic synthesizer in 1955). Trigger, Roy Rogers's horse – well, Leonard Slye's horse – was the former Golden Cloud. That was his name when Maid Marian (Marian Fitzwalter) rode him in *The Adventures of Robin Hood* (1938). He became Trigger after Rogers acquired him, and now that he (Trigger, that is) is stuffed and on display at the Double R Bar Ranch, it's likely the name will stick.

Some personalities have chosen to extend their names. "Lassie," for example, is a doubling of syllables from "Pal," her litter name. Then there's Joseph-Désiré Mobutu. After seizing power in Zaire in 1965, he officially changed his name to Mobutu Sese Seko Ngbendu wa Zabanga, "the all-powerful warrior whose endurance and inflexible will to win sweeps him from victory to victory leaving fire in his wake." (Nobody called him Joe.)

You probably know that the majority of first names in Western culture come from the Bible, although none of the 3,037 male first names or 181 female names in the Old and New Testaments is Gregory or Eldred. You can't find Pepsi or Cola in the Bible either, but both appear as first names on birth certificates issued in Pennsylvania in 1979.

56

Q: This country is the world's largest exporter of wool. To produce it, the country tends the world's second largest sheep flock. What's the country?

A: Sure, Australia.

The Challenge

Q: What country tends the world's largest sheep flock?

A: **China**, which also outnumbers Australia in pig and goat count. Not that this upsets the Australians too much, for they can claim the world's longest fence. It runs continuously for 3,307 miles (5,291 km), from Yalata in the state of South Australia to Jandowae in Queensland. That's quite a bit longer than the Great Wall of China at 2,550 miles (4,100 km). However, the Chinese wall is definitely doing its job today: keeping out invading hordes of Mongols, Tartars, and other aggressive nomads. Australians acknowledge that their fence, erected for the sole purpose of keeping wild dingo dogs away from the sheep, has a somewhat more porous record.

Sheep once filled the White House lawn in 1917. Woodrow Wilson arranged for a flock to keep the grass down so gardeners could be freed up for military service. The venture was, by all accounts, a good news/bad news undertaking. Although the president enthusiastically pointed to the vast amounts of "White House wool" being generated for the Red Cross, the very active digestive systems of these ovine imports made strolling on the grounds such an adventure that some of the released gardeners had to be replaced by workers with other, albeit simpler, skills.

During Eisenhower's term, bureaucrats briefly considered a Great Wall or Australian fence for the White House lawn, when hordes of squirrels interfered with the president's putting practice. But neither the Wilsons nor the Eisenhowers had to contend with the frustrations of John and Abigail Adams. Like most residents of Washington, they had to contend with wandering pigs on what wasn't even a lawn yet. But it's hard to believe Abigail was stressed by anything that ordinary. She was, after all, the first First Lady to hang laundry in the East Room.

57

Q: Millions of these instruments lie on desks or stand in cups. Sometimes they're seen in shirt pockets, or behind ears, even in people's mouths. Most of them are painted yellow, and many have the letters HB stamped on them? What are these instruments?

A: Of course, lead pencils.

The Challenge

Q: Surely you saw this coming: What does HB mean?

A: **Hard Black.** In lead pencils, hardness and blackness are determined by the ratio of clay to graphite. The more clay, the harder the lead (and the lighter the mark); the more graphite, the softer (but blacker). Art pencils usually have a B rating (8B is softest) and drafting pencils an H rating (up to 10H). HB is where the two scales overlap.

There has never been any lead in a lead pencil, by the way. When graphite was discovered (in England, 1564), it was called plumbago ("acts like lead") but soon became known as "black lead" in common parlance. The first English pencils were made by wrapping string around a stick of graphite, to be unraveled as needed. Germany was first to put the graphite in slender pieces of wood, and it was the French, faced with a graphite shortage in the Seven Years War, who came up with a clay mix in 1765.

A pencil is called a pencil because of its resemblance to the pencillium, a writing brush made by shaping a cluster of animal hairs inside a hollow reed. (It worked not unlike a modern mechanical pencil.) Until graphite took over, the pencillium and the quill pen were the writing instruments of choice. The new device became popular very quickly. It was clean, simple, and most of all sturdy.

That was not the case for the next major writing breakthrough — typewriters. Eliphalet Remington's company first marketed these devices successfully in 1874, but they were prone to jamming if used at high speed. To slow down typists, therefore, Remington & Sons cleverly scattered the most used letters all over the keyboard. That illogical design became the standard and still is today.

58

Q: This fictional lawman appeared first on radio, in 1933. Then in rapid order came movies, a movie serial, a comic strip, a mound of pulp novels, and a TV series that debuted on ABC in 1949. In all these media nobody ever addressed him by a name — not even with "Hey, Lone Ranger!" — except for his faithful Indian companion. What did Tonto call the Lone Ranger?

A: Sure, Kemo Sabe.

The Challenge

Q: What does *Kemo Sabe* mean?

A. **In Navajo, it means "soggy shrub"**; in Apache, "white shirt"! (The producers of the radio show intended it to mean "faithful friend.")

It gets better. *Tonto*, in Spanish, means "stupid." Whether or not that was an intentional choice by the producers, Tonto did spend the first set of radio shows without his own horse, riding double behind the Lone Ranger. His dialogue also suffered badly at the hands of the script writers – e.g., "Him take-um horse, Kemo Sabe." – contributing mightily to the widespread but erroneous belief that all native people speak English this way.

Should your next cocktail party include someone with a doctorate in linguistics and a passionate interest in cowboy culture (or the other way around), you might stir things by observing that it's highly unlikely Tonto would have spoken Navajo or Apache, or Spanish, because in the biography created for his character, his people are the Potawatomi, members of the Ojibway Federation, whose traditional territory is half a continent away from "Hi-ho Silver" territory.

The name Silver, by the way, has enjoyed an impressive shelf life as a horse moniker. Before the Lone Ranger came along, a popular movie cowboy of the 1920s had a white stallion named Silver King. In B westerns, Sunset Carson rode a Silver, while in very B movies, Whip Wilson rode Silver Bullet. Thomas J. Smith, first marshal of Abilene, Kansas (for real; he was Wild Bill Hickok's predecessor), had a horse named Silverheels, which trivia buffs will immediately recognize as the surname of the actor who played Tonto in the TV series. That was Jay Silverheels, a Mohawk from Canada who left a promising career in professional lacrosse to take the role. His real name was Harry Smith.

59

Q: Conductor Sir Thomas Beecham said of this musical instrument that it sounds the same after you have learned to play it as it did when you first started. Both maligned and adored, the instrument is strongly associated with Scotland, even though it's very international. The instrument?

A: Of course, the bagpipe. And it *is* bagpipe, incidentally, not bagpipes; you only get bagpipes when more than one are skirling.

The Challenge

Q: How many pipes are there on a Scottish bagpipe?

A: **Four.** A chanter, a breather, and two drones. (Irish pipes have three drones.) Aficionados with in-depth bagpipe background at hand — e.g., the ancient Roman name for it (*tibia utricularis*), or the fact that Leopold Mozart wrote a symphony for bagpipe, hurdy-gurdy, and strings in 1755 — might argue that the chanter and breather are not actually pipes. That's a quibble, though, something to be expected when an instrument has been around for such a long time.

Notable in the checkered history of the bagpipe is its use by the Gurkha regiments of Nepal to scare the enemy before a charge. How effective the Gurkhas found it might be measured by a 1996 decree from the European Soccer Association, which put bagpipes on a list of banned weapons, along with knives, fireworks, and gasoline canisters! Still, there is no record of anyone ever being killed by a bagpipe. (Unlike the didgeridoo, once used for just that purpose in Australia. See *Regina vs Long Harry*, killing of Kevin Frog: Darwin, 1979.)

As for the opinion of Sir Thomas Beecham, the reputation of the bagpipe has indeed undergone cycles of ups and downs. The fact that there's a word for bagpipe in over three dozen languages and dialects certainly proclaims its widespread use. However, one of the German dialect words for bagpipe, *dudelsack*, also means "to play an instrument badly." Speaking of Germans: In 1942, writing from his temporary cell in the Tower of London, Rudolf Hess told his wife that although he admired the quality of drill by the troops stationed there, he could have done without the bagpipes.

60

Q: Elizabeth II (her father called her Lillibet) was Elizabeth Windsor until the day in 1947 when she married Prince Philip. She was still a princess then, and Philip wasn't even a prince, but she still took his surname when they married. What is it?

A: Right, Mountbatten.

The Challenge

Q: After her coronation in 1953, Elizabeth changed her surname yet again. (This is not all that hard to do when you're queen.) What did she change it to?

A: **Back to Windsor.** Technically, royals are identified by a dynastic name, similar to but not precisely the same as the surnames used by us plebs. Usually, a dynastic name ends upon the death of a queen. Thus, after Queen Victoria died in 1901 (she was Victoria Hanover), her son Edward VII took on his father's German dynasty name, Saxe-Coburg. That made for terrible PR in World War I, so in 1917 Edward's son George V issued a royal decree changing the name to Windsor (prompting a rare witticism from Kaiser Wilhelm II, who announced he would be going to the theater now to see performances of *The Merry Wives of Saxe-Coburg*).

Queen Elizabeth's reversion to Windsor was apparently on the advice of Winston Churchill, who argued for the importance of dynastic continuity, even though the surname Mountbatten has a resonance all its own in England. Philip, who had been born a Schleswig-Holstein-Sonderburg-Glucksburg on his father's side, had picked Mountbatten, one of his mother's family names, when he became a British subject. This happened in 1947, just in time for the wedding. (Born in Corfu, he was originally a citizen of Greece.) Philip didn't do all that badly with the switch. He was made duke of Edinburgh on the eve of the wedding and ten years later was made a prince.

Also ordering new stationery at about the same time as Her Majesty was movie star Diana Dors, one of the more prominent mammary marvels in movies of the 1950s. She had been born Diana Fluck. There is no evidence, however, that her name change was undertaken on the advice of Winston Churchill.

61

Q: It would not be fair to call this temperance work a pot-boiler, but you could call it a pot stirrer. When it appeared in 1854, it became an immediate bestseller and stayed that way for years. You probably haven't read it, but you likely know the title. It's Timothy Shay Arthur's *Ten Nights in a* . . . Ten nights in a what?

A: Yes, a barroom. The full title is *Ten Nights in a Barroom and What I Saw There*. As a bestseller, however, Arthur's book remained a slightly lagging, if respectable, number three throughout its time, never quite managing to bump the Bible and one other book out of the two top spots.

The Challenge

Q: What is the title of the other book?

A: *Uncle Tom's Cabin, or Life Among the Lowly*, by Harriet Beecher Stowe. It appeared on March 20, 1852, and sold a million in sixteen months. At first, Stowe readily acknowledged that her idea for Uncle Tom came from the experiences of Josiah Henson, a runaway slave from Maryland who escaped to Canada via the Underground Railroad in 1830 and nineteen years later published a seventy-six-page autobiography. After her novel's great success, however, Stowe was given to more lofty attributions, maintaining, "God wrote it. I merely wrote His dictation."

However a perusal of Stowe's other writing suggests that, most of the time, her sources were somewhat more earthbound. Even earthy. In 1869, strictly on the word of ex-Lady Byron, who had been summarily dumped after a year of marriage to the famous poet, Stowe accused the flamboyant, and long dead, Byron of incest with his sister. This article and a host of other titles you have never heard of fill her collected works.

Compared to Stowe, Timothy Shay Arthur was entirely without ambivalence. He wanted to rehabilitate the world. His high-caliber hyperbole was directed at not just alcohol but smoking, gambling, business speculation, materialism, mesmerism, and credit buying. Strangely, though, his ethical canon had room for dancing and card-playing.

This didn't bother the censors in Russia, it seems. Throughout the 1850s, a fanatical level of censorship prevailed there under Nicholas I. All newly written music, for example, was scrutinized for subversive messages. Likewise, all newly published books, in both original language and translation, had to pass muster. *Uncle Tom's Cabin* was banned on first read. *Ten Nights in a Barroom*, however, made the cut.

62

Q: What does it mean to be faced with "Hobson's choice"?

A: Exactly, there's no choice at all; one option only.

The Challenge

Q: There really was a Hobson. What profession or occupation did he follow that would earn him such a legacy?

A: **He ran a livery stable and an inn.** It helps that he did it in Cambridge, England, where John Milton was a student (Christ's College). Milton wrote an epitaph for Hobson when he died.

The apparently very testy Thomas (a.k.a. Tobias) Hobson (1544–1631) was well known for rigorously enforcing his livery stable rule that renters could pick any horse, so long as it was the one nearest the door.

There is a street in Cambridge named after Hobson, which suggests that his enterprise was not blamed in the many complaints seen in old city records for the amount of horse dung on the local thoroughfares. However, the situation could not have been all that bad, for those same records offer no indication that young people of the city ever took up road hockey with any enthusiasm. But then, this spontaneous street game never caught on in New York City either, where by 1900 the streets hosted two and a half million pounds of the stuff daily, and avoiding it, one might fairly assume, would have been a preoccupation of the typical pedestrian. Brooklyn's first major baseball team was called the Trolley Dodgers, but locals knew better.

Aside from embracing Hobson's legacy, Cambridge University has generated some important data for the world to use in its planning for daily life. In a controlled experiment in 1982, for example, researchers determined that only one out of eight randomly selected rats would choose a Mars Bar over cheddar cheese if given the (un-Hobson) choice. Undergrads there have also calculated that since 1923 the quantity of street-surface horse dung in Europe has declined at a rate 15% slower, on average, than in North America.

Q: During the twentieth century only two computers ever became well-known personalities. One is real: Deep Blue. It took on chess grandmaster Gary Kasparov in 1996 (and lost) and 1997 (and won). The other is fictional. It starred in Stanley Kubrick's 1968 movie, *2001: A Space Odyssey*. What is this fictional computer's name?

A: Right, Hal. (Actually, H A L 9000.)

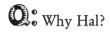

The Challenge

Q: Why Hal?

A: HAL is IBM backed up one alphabet position.

IBM was not first off the mark with the computer. Most techno-geeks know that English mathematician Charles Babbage designed one in the 1830s. Perhaps because it called for steam power, his design never resulted in an actual CPU, which was too bad for a contemporary mathematician, William Shanks. He spent fifteen years hand-figuring the value of pi to 707 decimal places. In 1949, when the first electronic computers tried calculating it (to 2,035 places in three days), they showed that Shanks had goofed at about the 600th place — which threw off his last three years of work!

Shanks was an avid chess player. So was Austrian music teacher and charlatan extraordinaire Johann Maelzel (1772–1838), developer of the "panharmonicon," his name for a weird sort of calliope. A smoothie, though. He convinced Beethoven to write *Wellington's Victory* for it, and the two went on tour briefly before falling out. Maelzel's *pièce de résistance*, however, was "the Turk," a chessboard held by a huge statue of a Turk, who took on volunteers from an audience. Whenever Maelzel opened the Turk's chest, a complex array of gears, shafts, and pulleys could be seen whirring away while a wooden arm moved the chess pieces with uncanny intelligence. Maelzel fled Vienna with the Turk in 1825, and for two years had a great run wowing North American audiences, until he was exposed one night in Baltimore. That night, when the curtain closed, two boys peering through a knothole saw a small man crawl out of the statue's capacious insides. It didn't take long to identify European chess bum William Schlumberger and bring an end to Maelzel's colorful career.

Spectators of Kasparov's games with Deep Blue say he has never once tried to peek inside his opponent.

Q: "Lizzie Borden took an ax,
And gave her mother forty whacks.
When she saw what she had done,
She gave her father . . ."

How many?

A: Yes, forty-one.

The Challenge

Q: Did she really do it?

A: **No, according to a jury.** On August 4, 1892, in Falls River, MA, Lizzie's stepmother and father were murdered (nineteen and ten whacks respectively) and Lizzie was charged. She had bought a small ax on August 3. It was she who discovered the bodies (her sister was out of town), and she had been seen burning a dress similar to the one she was wearing on the fateful day. Lizzie didn't help herself either by offering two different alibis.

At the trial, one of Lizzie's attorneys, a former governor of the state, argued convincingly that the time frame made it impossible for her to be guilty. The police had lost their map of the crime-scene blood spatters, and in 1892 the only police force in the world capable of using fingerprint evidence was in Buenos Aires. Throughout the proceedings, Lizzie was such a picture of prim innocence that, in closing argument, her lawyer was able to say to the jury, "Gentlemen, to find Lizzie Borden guilty, you must believe she is a fiend. Does she look it?" Apparently not. Unanimous acquittal came in sixty-six minutes.

Although Lizzie's eccentric father was wealthy, the Bordens lived in a rundown part of town in a house with neither gaslight nor bathtub. (This too led to suspicion, because Lizzie was scrubbed clean when she reported discovery of the bodies.) Family members customarily avoided one another, shutting themselves in separate rooms except at mealtimes, although given the breakfast on August 4 – mutton broth, rotten bananas, johnnycake, cookies, and coffee – eating may not have been a high point either. Lizzie and her sister lived a much more pleasant life with their inheritance. When she passed away in 1927, Lizzie left an estate of over a million dollars.

◁ **65** ▷

Q: Unless you are the one person in 500 who is allergic to aspirin, you have likely taken it at some time or other. It's an acid, and although you might have trouble spelling it, you know its name. What is it?

A: Sure, acetylsalicylic acid, still one of the world's most widely used painkillers and anti-inflammatory medications.

The Challenge

Q: In what country was aspirin discovered?

A: Not Germany, but France. In 1853, chemist Charles Gerhardt synthesized acetylsalicylic acid at the University of Montpellier, but didn't think much of it and shelved his work. Forty years later, at the Bayer company in Germany, chemist Felix Hoffman was desperate to relieve his father's agony from arthritis. He knew about Gerhardt and was willing to give anything a shot. The rest, as they say . . .

In 1919, Bayer lost the Aspirin trademark as part of war reparation payments. Drug companies then conducted a war of their own until a 1921 court decision ruled that Aspirin is aspirin, and nobody can own the name.

Throughout all this entanglement, Bayer was having quite a nice time with a syrup in which a principal ingredient was heroin. First marketed internationally in 1898 (a year before Aspirin) as a cough medicine, by 1906 it was being recommended by the AMA as a painkiller. When North America banned importation in 1924, the syrup had thousands of regular customers whose cough was well under control but who kept pretending otherwise.

By this time, Coca Cola was no longer an alternative for consumers seeking a buzz. When John Styth Pemberton first brewed up the concoction (registered in 1885 as "French Wine Coca – Ideal Nerve and Tonic Stimulant") in his back yard, he included cocaine and caffeine. Coke still uses coca (minus the lift) and, optionally, the kola nut, which has caffeine, but thrill seekers, if they wish to stay inside the law, have to be more creative now. Whether or not former San Francisco policeman Dan White qualifies as one of these is open to debate. In 1978, he shot the city mayor and a councillor. A jury accepted his plea of temporary insanity caused by an overconsumption of Hostess Twinkies!

66

Q: What game of chance, requiring only a pair of dotted cubes and a flat surface, has the best payout rate of all forms of legalized gambling?

A: Yes, craps. According to *Consumers Research Magazine*, craps pays out at a rate of 98%.

The Challenge

Q: What form of legalized gambling has the *worst* payout rate?

A. **Lotteries.** On average, their payout rate is 49%. Slots pay out in the 75–95% range. The racetrack pays 83–87% of the time. Jai alai is a little finer (85–87%), while roulette averages 95%.

These percentages could be related to the amount of brain power required, as a California anti-gambling group once demonstrated by training a chimpanzee to operate a slot machine in a single twenty-minute session. (She lost money.) The same chimp played roulette and craps (winning at both) but couldn't figure out the betting on jai alai or the ponies. She never did buy a lottery ticket.

Arguably, lotteries can be approached with strategy, albeit sledgehammer-style. An Australian investment club tried to buy all seven million tickets for sale in the February 1992 Virginia state lottery. When the bell rang, the club had acquired only five million, but that was enough to win top prize, a $1.3-million annual dividend for twenty years. A clumsy scheme, but somewhat brighter than the one adopted by a bank robber in Montreal in 1976. In addition to grabbing cash, he scooped up a pile of unsold lottery tickets, one of which, a few days later, was a half-million-dollar winner. He tried to collect and ended up with a thirteen-year holiday in the slammer.

As a service to readers who live in lottery hope and plan to win big without breaking the law, here are some data which may help their planning. During the first ten years of Canada's Lotto 6/49, which pays out several million dollars twice a week, the following six numbers came up most frequently — but not necessarily at the same time: 31 (most frequent by far), then, in order, 7, 43, 47, 34, and 32. The six least frequently appearing, in order: 15, 48, 12, 6, 2, and 10.

67

Q: The most famous paintings of George Washington are his five full-length portraits by Gilbert Stuart, and one that depicts him committing a nautical safety violation that, for Washington, would have been completely out of character. What is the title of this last painting?

A: Sure, *Washington Crossing the Delaware* (on December 25, 1776), painted by Emmanuel Leutze around 1850. It shows Washington standing up in an overcrowded boat in bad weather, not at all typical behavior for the first president.

The Challenge

Q: He's not crossing the Delaware either. What river does Leutze depict in this painting?

A: **The Rhine.** It's a reasonable use of artistic license, since Leutze did the painting in Dusseldorf. But he didn't stop there. The boat is the wrong size and type, and the thirteen stars and stripes flag hadn't yet been adopted when Washington made that crossing. Artist Gilbert Stuart is no innocent either. To establish an image he felt would be more appropriate, he convinced Washington to stuff cotton in his cheeks during the official sittings. The former president had lost all his teeth by then, and both his wooden and his metal dentures, apparently, were a cosmetic failure. Yet his cheeks were so sunken without them that he appeared emaciated.

With the exception of quotations wrongly attributed to Abraham Lincoln and inventions credited to Benjamin Franklin, George Washington is probably the subject of more fables than any other American. A favorite, but with a grain of truth, is his alleged throwing of a coin across the Potomac. The grain, according to his cousins, is that George was wont to throw, not coins, but stones. (Throwing coins away would have been as out of character as standing up in a boat.) And he threw them across, not the Potomac, but another Virginia river, the Rappahannock.

This story was more or less confirmed by a media setup in 1936, in which yet another legend, former big league fastballer Walter "Big Train" Johnson, heaved a silver dollar across the Rappahannock, with distance to spare, at about the point where Washington would have – if he really did. Worth noting is that at the time, Johnson, although retired for some years, still held the record for most wild pitches in the majors. *Washington Crossing the Delaware* has hung in the Metropolitan Museum of Art in New York since 1897, but it's now a replica. The original was destroyed by Allied bombing in 1943.

68

Q: The first chemical compound, complete with formula, that most students learn about is H_2O – water. This makes sense, because water is the most common compound in the universe, and it's made up of the first and third most common elements. Which is the first?

A: Yes, hydrogen is the most common, and oxygen is the third.

The Challenge

Q: What's the second?

A: **Helium**, first discovered by Sir Joseph Lockyer in England, and by Pierre Janssen of France, both in 1868. Lockyer was a clerk in the War Office but 1868 was a slow year – just a brief invasion of Ethiopia – so presumably he was able to take long lunches and look for helium. Janssen was far more frenetic: Peru in 1857–58 to determine the magnetic equator; Italy in 1861–64 to study telluric rays; and the Azores in 1867 for topographic studies – all before the helium.

Hydrogen too is a shared discovery, first distinguished from other flammable gases by Sir Henry Cavendish in 1776 but only named as an element by Antoine Lavoisier in 1781 (which makes one wonder what Cavendish called it). A wealthy and truly nutty recluse, Cavendish also discovered the composition of nitric acid, isolated argon (without realizing it), and anticipated much of the work of the great Michael Faraday.

The discovery of oxygen (1774) is traditionally credited to Joseph Priestley, a workaholic Presbyterian minister, early exponent of Unitarianism, and teacher of anatomy, astronomy, modern history, and general science. Unfortunately, Priestley has suffered somewhat from revisionism. Karl Scheele of Sweden beat him to oxygen by a good two years. Priestley's explanation of the discharge from a Leyden jar proved to be not quite on the money. And, contrary to received wisdom, he did not coin the phrase, "greatest happiness for the greatest number." On the plus side, Priestley's discovery of how to decompose ammonia with electricity has held up. Also, it was he who discovered, in 1878, that graphite marks on paper can be erased with congealed sap from a rubber tree. Too bad he didn't live long enough to see American inventor Hyman Lipman come up with the idea, in 1858, of attaching the stuff to the end of a lead pencil.

69

Q: What book did Johannes Gutenberg print in c. 1450 using movable type?

A: Yes, the Bible, or, as it is more popularly known, the Gutenberg Bible.

The Challenge

Q: In what language was it printed?

A: **Latin.** Three hundred copies were printed in Mainz, in what is now Germany, between 1451 and 1456.

Gutenberg was not first off the mark with movable type. That happened in Korea in 1409. He was, however, likely the first in Europe to print a book in the vernacular: *Appeal of Christianity Against the Turks* (1454). The first movable-type production in English was William Caxton's *The Recuyell of the Histories of Troye* (c. 1474), which he blithely lifted from a French manuscript. In his preface Caxton proudly states, "[This book] is not wreton with penne and ynke as other bokes ben . . . [but was] begonne in oon day, and also fynysshid in oon day," thus laying claim to being the first – and quite possibly the last – printer in history ever to bring a job in on time.

Gutenberg's first printing of the Bible seems awfully tiny, but in publishing, it's customary to print small and hope big. Sometimes that works. Since 1815, the Bible has had a run of close to seven billion copies in 2,919 languages and dialects. Sometimes it doesn't work. The first print run of *How to Test Your Urine at Home* (Haldeman-Julius, 1935), by B.C. Meyrowitz, never did sell out. Nor did Alfred Rose's *Build Your Own Hindenburg* (Putnam, 1983), and Hal Cory's *Wall-Paintings by Snake Charmers in Tanganyika* (Faber & Faber, 1953) wasn't exactly a barnburner either. Prospects for would-be authors (or their estates) are not all bleak, however. E. Micklethwaite Curr's *Recollections of Squatting in Victoria*, first seen in 1883 (500 copies), was reprinted by Melbourne University Press in 1965.

70

Q: To find the Channel Islands, you'd look in an atlas (or, if you happen to be in a boat, you might try the northwest coast of France). To find *Islands in the Stream*, where would you look?

A: Right, in a library or a bookstore. You would likely find it in a video rental store too, for Hemingway's novel has also been made into a movie.

The Challenge

Q: Where would you look for the islands of Langerhans?

A: **In your pancreas.** They are cells that secrete insulin. Pathologist Paul Langerhans discovered them around 1880.

Over forty years passed before Canadians Frederick Banting and Charles Best refined insulin to combat diabetes. Yet in historical terms, that passage of time is a mere blink. Right up to the end of the nineteenth century, medical practice was still very much based on the 2,000-year-old concepts of Hippocrates and Galen. There were exceptions, of course, like Edward Jenner, who in 1796 turned the Western world on its ear when he inoculated eight-year-old James Phipps with liquid taken from pustules on a milkmaid's hands. Nevertheless, for centuries physicians continued to follow the practice of "bleeding *ad deliquim animi*" (draw blood until they faint), along with purging, semi-starvation, and two popular but terrifying therapies, deliberate blistering (as awful as it sounds) and cupping (where the patient's flesh is cut and a heated cup put over it; the resulting vacuum draws blood).

One problem was communication. Joseph Lister had introduced antisepsis in 1860, but many surgeons continued to use dressings made from pressed sawdust because they just didn't know about Lister's work. Another problem was acceptance. At almost the same time, Ignaz Semmelweis in Austria and Oliver Wendell Holmes *père* in America argued for antiseptic procedures during childbirth. Holmes made real headway, while Semmelweis was drummed out of the club. Still, there is a place for conservatism. In the southern U.S., around 1910, an epileptic suffering daily seizures was bitten by a rattlesnake and the seizures stopped completely. When this phenomenon was published in a medical journal, rattlesnake venom suddenly became a hot cure. More careful research revealed that in all but a very few cases, the venom just made epileptics sick.

Q: Although New York City boosters, especially those in the tourist office, prefer "Big Apple," for many years the city has had another nickname. Among other comic book characters, Batman and Robin helped make that name popular. What is it?

A: Right, Gotham, sometimes Gotham City.

The Challenge

Q: Who gave New York City that name?

A: **Washington Irving.** The creator of Ichabod Crane and Rip Van Winkle meant it satirically, for he felt that New York was pretty much a madhouse. And that was back in 1807!

Irving's dig comes from Gotham, in Nottinghamshire, England – Robin Hood country – where the villagers once feigned mass madness to deter King John from building a residence.

Ironically, "Gotham" has taken on a somewhat complimentary tone, meaning biggest of the big. Thus Irving would no doubt be reassured to know that madness in New York is still alive and well. Take the "Super Bowl toilet flush" for example. On the Friday preceding Super Bowl XXI, local Environmental Commissioner Harvey Schultz issued a warning that if all New Yorkers chose the natural and opportune halftime break to use the can, the city's water pressure would collapse. It was later acknowledged as a gag, but belief in this danger persists. So does the story, reported in the *New York Times* on February 10, 1935, that the city's sewers are host to abandoned alligators, flushed down as unwanted pets. What would likely please Irving most is a survey of subway passengers in the 1970s revealing that "please" or "thank-you" is heard from three out of every ten riders in Hamburg, Germany, from five out of every ten in Tokyo, seven in London, and in New York, one.

Gotham City Trust & Savings is the bank from which John Beresford Tipton drew checks on *The Millionaire* (delivered by Michael Anthony). And if that stirs a memory, you likely know that on *The Honeymooners*, Ralph Kramden drove for the Gotham Bus Company.

Q: What color is the fish that throws everyone off track during a discussion or a meeting?

A: Right, red. It's a "red herring." This piscatorial metaphor has been part of the English language for centuries.

The Challenge

Q: Why red?

A: **When it is dried, salted, and smoked, a herring turns red** – and supersmelly. Definitely something you don't leave in your backpack overnight. The saying originates in medieval times, when herring were used to train hounds for stag hunting.

Color metaphors tend to live a varied life across different languages. Someone "in the red" in English is "in the green" in Italian. An off-color story (Why are there no "on-color" stories?) is green in Spanish but blue in English. Depending on what source you choose to believe, the risqué quality of blue comes either from the blue pencils of censors or from the fact that Chinese brothels were painted blue to make them distinctive. In French, a blue story is a fairy tale, while in German it's a fib. (If nothing else, this suggests that citizens of these two countries behaved themselves better than the English while visiting the Far East.) An interesting exception is purple, which in most languages has enjoyed an almost exclusive use in metaphors for royalty. The reason, we are told, is rarity. Until a synthetic dye was developed in 1856, the only way, worldwide, to get purple dye was by applying pressure to the anal glands of a certain tiny Mediterranean shellfish. Royals, obviously, were pretty much the only group that could afford to pay surrogate squeezers.

While hounds in pursuit can be distracted by a red herring, a similar result cannot be guaranteed in the case of giraffes, unless the herring itself is left on the trail. Giraffes do not smell terribly well, but unlike fighting bulls, they can see the color red. Not green, yellow, or orange, though, for giraffes are semi-achromatopsic. That's still better than hamsters; they're completely achromatopsic. But then, hamsters are not much good at chasing foxes anyway.

Q: She once forgot the lyrics to a song during a live performance, and her recovery won her a Grammy. Who was this "First Lady of Song"?

A: Of course, Ella Fitzgerald.

The Challenge

Q: What was the song?

A. **"Mack the Knife,"** on which she improvised in Berlin in 1960. After saying to the audience, "I hope I remember all the words," she didn't, but the result is a jazz classic. (The album is *Ella in Berlin*.)

"Mack the Knife" has been recorded by many different artists but as a potential Guinness nominee for "most frequent" it's way back in the pack. Lennon and McCartney's "Yesterday" was recorded by others almost 1,200 times in its first eight years. "Tie a Yellow Ribbon 'Round the Old Oak Tree" took only six years to get to a similar number. "St. Louis Blues" (W. C. Handy, 1914) and "Stardust" (Hoagy Carmichael, 1927) are almost there, but they've taken much longer. And none of these numbers come even close to the industrial-level production of Lata Mangeshker, once the hottest female singer in India. Between 1948 and 1974, she laid down over 25,000 tracks in twenty different Indian languages.

As fly-right-off-the-shelf sellers, Ms. Mangeshker's records have never approached the level of *The Beatles*, a 1968 double LP which hit a sales figure of two million in its first week. Even that one is well back of *John Fitzgerald Kennedy – A Memorial Album*. In December 1963, this record sold four million copies (at 99 cents) in five days. Given the technology of the day, the producers must have begun on the very day of Kennedy's assassination.

The recording industry's smallest-ever discs were produced in 1923 by HMV. These playable records fit comfortably inside a toilet paper roll, and were made for Queen Mary's Doll House (now set up for viewing at Windsor Castle). HMV made 92,000, including 35,000 pressings of "God Save the King" (which forces the conclusion that the queen was either patriotic beyond measure or had very lousy equipment).

74

Q: What is this symbol [&] called?

A: Yes, it's an ampersand, and it substitutes for the word "and."

The Challenge

Q: What is this symbol [/] called?

A: **A virgule** (or solidus). It substitutes for "per," as in parts/ million, and for "or," as in has/has not. In the late twentieth century, it also had a brief and ignominious life as a gender-yoke, as in his/hersterectomy.

Symbols like virgules and ampersands, when they are used in text in place of words, are called grammalogs. Now, if you're planning to use that information in a singles bar, you should be aware that, despite universal agreement on their use as symbols, there is widespread disagreement over their names. Take the grammalog @, for example. In every language using @ in that form, it stands for "at." But the name for it varies dramatically. In Dutch and German, for example, it's called a spider monkey, but in Swiss German it's an *affen-schwanz* ("monkey's tail"). The French have it as a *commercial*, or sometimes *commercial A*, and in Spain, Portugal, and much of South America, it's an *arroba*, which is a unit of weight. The best, however, is English, where it has no name at all! Another gem is the octothorp [#], which voicemail systems call either a number sign or a pound key – despite the fact that the # is not a number sign unless it precedes a numeral (as in Suite #242) and is not a pound sign unless it follows a numeral (as in 40# keg of nails).

Thus, in a singles bar you're probably better to stick with jarns, nettles, grawlices, and quimps (comic-book swearing). Or you might want to use the proper name for the paragraph symbol: pilcrow. A printing imperfection, especially one caused by wrinkles in the paper, is called a mackle. You might also have luck with tittle. It's the dot over the letter i.

75

Q: One of those intriguing "first" claims that will never be verified absolutely is the one that insists the first genuine French kiss in a Hollywood movie made for general release was between Natalie Wood and Warren Beatty in 1961. What was the movie?

A: Sure, *Splendor in the Grass*, a film that stirred up a variety of passions following its release.

The Challenge

Q: Easier to verify is the first-ever kiss in a movie. It was between Canadian actress May Irwin and American actor John C. Rice. What was this movie?

A: *The Kiss*, shot in Thomas Edison's New Jersey studio in 1896. Audiences were shocked but they must have recovered, for only thirty years later, in *Don Juan*, John Barrymore divided 127 smackers between Mary Astor and Estelle Taylor (not evenly; Astor was the clear winner). Moviegoers in India had to wait until 1978 to see their first hot screen clutch. Shashi Kapoor delivered unto Zeenat Aman in *Love Sublime*, and stirred up a hornet's nest that even dragged in the government. This, in a nation that over a thousand years before gave us the *Kama Sutra*, arguably the world's first sex manual!

Almost all cultures are kissing ones. Notable exceptions have been the nose-rubbing Innu in the Arctic and several Polynesian groups in the Pacific. (The latter also enjoyed *mitakuku*, which involves mutual biting of eyebrow hair.) The Romans, by Julius Caesar's time, had taken up kissing in a big way, which may account for its popularity in the Western world. People in the Middle and Far East are kissers but it's much more ritualized, in both the manner of expression and the selection of kissee by kisser. Ritual kissing has also flourished in the West, especially the "air kiss" or "Park Avenue grunt" which Nancy Reagan raised to an art form.

Kissing has had some bad press, Judas Iscariot's story being a prime example, and some authoritative interference too. In 1311, Pope Clement V declared the act a mortal sin if the participants had stepped-up activity in mind. In 1652, Oliver Cromwell made it illegal on Sundays. But mostly, our leaders have wisely let custom control the issue. Not without a failure or two: In 1977, the poobahs of royal protocol at Buckingham Palace fainted *en masse* when, at a state ceremony, President Jimmy Carter kissed the Queen Mother on the lips.

76

Q: According to Genesis 8:7, Noah released a bird from the ark when it finally landed. What kind of bird was it?

A: Indeed, a raven, but it just flew around. It was seven days after that when he released a dove, but it came back because there was no place to settle. Seven days after that, Noah released the dove again, and this time it came back with a newly picked olive leaf.

The Challenge

Q: Where had the ark landed?

A: On a mountain in Ararat (not on *Mount* Ararat). There is a mound of misinformation about mountains. Case in point: Everest. The world's highest peak is named after Colonel Sir George Everest (1790–1866), surveyor general of India, who pronounced his name EVE-rest. Also, its official height has been toyed with ever since the first official readings in 1849, most recently in 1987 when a U.S. expedition climbing K2 in Pakistan – K2 is the former Mount Godwin-Austen – claimed its equipment showed K2 to be higher than Everest.

It all depends on how the measuring is done. From bottom to top, Mauna Kea in Hawaii is a good 4,500 feet (1,371 m) higher than Everest. The problem is, the bottom of Mauna Kea is on the floor of the Pacific Ocean. From another perspective, i.e., closest to the sun, Mount Chimborazo in the Ecuadorian Andes is higher too. Because the earth is not perfectly round but spheroid (Columbus was not stressed by this, and you should not be either), sea level at the equator is some fourteen miles (twenty-two km) farther from the center of the earth than at the North Pole. Thus, given their latitudes, Chimborazo sticks out into space two miles (3.2 km) farther than Everest.

Confusion also prevails over another famous mountain. Mount Sinai rises on the modern-day Sinai Peninsula, but whether or not it's the Sinai of Moses and the burning bush is uncertain, for another tradition has the biblical peak in a remote area of Saudi Arabia. It is there that the ancient monastery of Saint Catherine is located. And talk about remote: In 1946, the first outsider to call on the monastery in eight years discovered that the monks had not heard about World War II.

There is a Mount Ararat, by the way. It's the tallest mountain in Turkey. No question.

77

Q: We first heard "My name is Barbie" in 1959. Earlier in the decade, we were blessed with the Frisbee (1956), the Hula Hoop (1958), and, in 1955, a phenomenally popular system of interconnecting plastic building blocks from Denmark, known as what?

A: Indeed, Lego.

The Challenge

Q: What does *Lego* mean?

A: **"Play well,"** from the Danish *leg godt*. The official company history acknowledges that they were not aware, at first, that *lego* means "I peruse, put together" in Latin.

When Kirk Christiannsen began making toy binding bricks – out of wood – in 1934, his little company of six employees was making stepladders and ironing boards. Although he likely would not have predicted that 1997 would see fifty branches in twenty-nine countries, there was reason for optimism. Lincoln Logs had been doing well since 1916. Erector Sets (1913) were steady sellers. Competition from Slinky Toy and Silly Putty was eleven years away. Besides, his bricks gave children something to do while their parents played Scrabble (1931) and Bingo (1929), both Great Depression hits, like Monopoly (1933).

Still, there's always a risk with great ideas. Ask England's John Ward. His bra-warmer (patented 1988) has never really received the attention it perhaps deserves. Nor has his musical frying pan (same date: cooking time is controlled by a menu of songs in the handle; two choruses of "Moon River" and your eggs are ready to flip).

Successful inventors say it's all in the timing. Ferenc Kovacs of Budapest would likely agree. In 1989, just when he had invented a singing condom that plays Communist marching songs, along came *perestroika*. Unfortunately, he'd run out of development capital and couldn't change the music. That hasn't stopped him. In 1996, he opened a laugh kiosk in Budapest, widely held to be the world's gloomiest city. Kovacs stands inside and, for a fee, tells a joke. The fee varies, depending on how funny the customer wants him to be. So far it's not a big hit, but when Kirk Christiannsen first showed neighbors his binding bricks, they all told him to keep on making ironing boards.

78

Q: It was published in England in 1755. Its title is *A Dictionary of the English Language*, and it is the prodigious effort of one person, working alone. Who is the author of this famous "first" dictionary?

A: Yes, Samuel Johnson, known also as Dr. Johnson (1709–84). His dictionary wasn't the first to be published in England, but it was the first to reflect current usage.

The Challenge

Q: Who wrote the first dictionary in North America?

A: **Samuel Johnson Jr.** He was a teacher from Connecticut, and in 1788 compiled *A School Dictionary*. Noah Webster, at the time, was writing *A Brief History of Epidemic Pestilential Disease*. He didn't bring out *An American Dictionary of the English Language* until 1828.

The first English work to actually sport the word "dictionary" in its title appeared about 1227, but it was basically a list of Latin words for memorization. That practice, i.e., publishing Latin dictionaries for English use, continued for another 325 years, until Richard Huloet's *Abcdarium Anglico-Latinum pro Tyrunculis* in 1552, a translation dictionary pairing English and Latin words. (Today, an "abcdarian," pronounced a-b-c-darian, is a person fixated with alphabetical order.)

Before Samuel Johnson's mighty tome, dictionaries generally limited their efforts to what were perceived as troublesome words. The full title of Robert Cawdrey's 1604 effort covers the bases nicely: *A Table Alphabeticall, conteyning and teaching the true writing and understanding of hard usuall English wordes — gathered for the benefit and helpe of Ladies, Gentlewomen, or any other unskillful persons.* Johnson offered English as it is (or was), but even he couldn't resist editorial positioning. His definition of oats, for example, is "A grain, which in England is generally given to horses, but in Scotland supports the people."

Most of the world's 5,000 or so languages have an English translation dictionary today, although some are relatively recent. The Bohemian-English dictionary came out in 1876; the Mongolian-English lexicon didn't appear until 1953.

So you don't have to check: The most common letter in the English language is E; the most common words are the, of, and, and to, in that order. And the most dictionary entries are under the letter T.

156

79

Q: Throughout the American Civil War, Confederate soldiers regularly sang two patriotic songs on their way into battle. One of them was "The Bonnie Blue Flag." You surely know the other one; what was it?

A: Yes, "Dixie."

The Challenge

Q: What is the song's published title?

A: **"I Wish I Was in Dixie's Land."** The C.S.A. had an anthem too: "God Save the South." It never really caught on, but then, very few anthems ever do. An obvious exception is *"La Marseillaise"*; however, it was written not as an anthem but as a marching song. Originally called the "War Song of the Army of the Rhine," it was so successful at cranking up passions that Napoleon banned it. It was not reinstated until 1879.

"God Save the King" is popular too, possibly because it has cycled through the British Empire, and also because its melody has been used for patriotic songs in Germany, Russia, Sweden, Liechtenstein, and the U.S.A. Like the U.S. national anthem, "God Save the King" is notorious for causing unconscious swaying, but that's no surprise, for both melodies were written in waltz tempo. The British anthem, however, at only fourteen bars long, usually escapes the interpretive battering that pop stars give "The Star-Spangled Banner." So does Iceland's anthem. Written by Matthias Jochumsson and Sveinbjorn Sveinbjornsson, it's a modest twenty-two bars. (And fortunately, neither writer tried to work his name into the lyrics.) At only eleven bars, Japan's anthem is a favorite of Olympic Games planners. On the other hand, they're terrified of Ecuador's. Including intro and choruses, it covers 135 bars, so that conceivably, a really hot, medal-producing team from Ecuador could extend the Olympics by nearly a day.

Some anthems are distinguished by having no lyrics at all. Bhutan, Mauritania, and Equatorial Guinea come to mind. Spain's has no words either. That was no help at all to King Alfonso XIII (1886–1941), who was so tone-deaf he couldn't even distinguish his country's anthem from general ambient noise. As a consequence, his formal entourage always included an "anthem man" to cue him when to stand up.

80

Q: When officials made a final check of the Oscars just before the Academy Awards in 1937, they noticed that the statuette slated for the winner of Best Actor was inscribed with the name of a comic-book character. This character is married to Tess Trueheart and they have an adopted son named Junior. Who is he?

A: Sure, Dick Tracy.

The Challenge

Q: The goof was corrected in time. Who got the award?

A: **Spencer Tracy**, for his role in *Captains Courageous*. It was a minor error, really, compared to mistakes in the films the Oscars celebrate. Sometimes the goofs are obvious, such as the blind man wearing a watch in *The Ten Commandments* (1956), Adolf Hitler's first name spelled "Adolph" in *Indiana Jones and the Last Crusade* (1989), and the label on Christ's robe in *The Last Temptation of Christ* (1988). Other times, you have to watch for them. In *The English Patient* (1996), Ralph Fiennes's fingernails are still nicely buffed and polished after he digs himself and Kristin Scott Thomas out of a mound of sand. Another that slipped by is Jimmy Stewart's cast in *Rear Window* (1954), which switches legs in one scene. In *The Godfather* (1972), Michael Corleone shoots the police chief in the neck, but if you watch carefully, you'll see the bullet hole is in his forehead! Maybe he wasn't supposed to be dead — like the corpse that blinks in *The Abyss* (1989).

Even landmark movies do it. Without reloading, Robert Redford fires seventeen shots from his two six-guns in *Butch Cassidy and the Sundance Kid* (1969). If you watch Peter Lorre's chest the next time you take home *The Maltese Falcon* (1941), you'll see his tie change inexplicably from polka dots to stripes. *Driving Miss Daisy* (1989) uses a Styrofoam cup, years before it was invented.

There's a long history of error in the arts, a tradition established well before Hollywood. Renaissance master Tintoretto (1518–94), in his painting *Israelites Gathering Manna in the Wilderness*, depicts Moses' companions with shotguns slung over their arms. To be fair to Tintoretto, we should point out that in his *Circumcision*, which hangs in the Church of Santa Maria del Carmine in Venice, the utensils at hand are both temporally and surgically correct.

81

Q: She was born Margaretha Zelle, on August 7, 1876. When she died by firing squad, on October 15, 1917, German intelligence was calling her "H-21." Both her birth name and her code number have pretty much disappeared into the mists of time, but not the name under which she performed exotic dances. Who was this dancer/courtesan/spy?

A: Yes, Mata Hari.

The Challenge

Q: What nationality was she?

A: Dutch. She was born in Holland, and moved to Java when she married. Back in Europe by 1905, and dancing in Paris salons, she claimed to be from India and said her name, Mata Hari, meant "eye of the dawn." Her dances, she added, had never before been seen outside Indian temples. They were, in fact, adapted from Javanese bayas performed in Buddhist, not Hindu, temples, but that was irrelevant to the mesmerized males in her audiences, who filled every seat each night to watch her strip to the almost buff. (She never went topless, claiming that her husband had disfigured her.)

Mata Hari became a spy around 1910 – for the Germans, principally because they were the first to ask. By all accounts, she was very effective; not surprising, given that she was performing privately for the French minister of foreign affairs, the French minister of war, the German foreign minister, the German crown prince, and the prime minister of Holland, all more or less at the same time! Among her coups was warning the German High Command about a new British weapon, the "land ship" (tank).

Most scholarly reviews of espionage conclude that the use of spies reached its apex in World War I, and that since that time high-tech spying, such as the kind that tracked Che Guevera in 1967, has produced better results. (To relieve his asthma in the jungle, Che used a portable wood stove. The infrared light was picked up by U-2 spyplanes.) Yet, given the alleged failures of the CIA to get rid of Fidel Castro by exotic means, one wonders.

Castro was once a pitching prospect for the Washington Senators. He was also an extra in Hollywood, and even shows up in Esther Williams's *Bathing Beauties*. Never did much as an exotic dancer, though.

Q: If you are a golfer, this is easy. Even if you are not, you can resort to logic. What are the little indentations on a golf ball called? (We are asking about the manufactured indentations, not the gouges that mysteriously appear after the ball is used.)

A: Yes, they're called dimples.

The Challenge

Q: How many are there?

A: **332.** Their normal depth is 0.013 inches (0.3 millimeters).

Dimples came about in the 1850s, when the gutta-percha or "guttie" ball replaced the leather ball, which was stuffed with feathers. Rubber-cored balls, known as "bounding bullies," first appeared in 1898, and the tee showed up a year after that.

The origin of golf itself is usually traced to Scotland, but evidence is vague. The Romans played *paganica* with a bent stick and a leather ball stuffed with feathers. The Chinese have long claimed that they played before the Romans. And the Dutch played *kolven* on frozen rivers and canals. (Putting must have been interesting.) Nevertheless, the Mecca of golf is in Scotland, namely the Royal and Ancient Golf Club of Saint Andrews. It was this course that in 1764 established eighteen holes as a standard. Prior to that, Saint Andrews had eleven holes in a straight line along the seacoast, so that a "round" of golf, out and back, was twenty-two holes.

The first U.S. course is believed to be a six-hole effort laid out in Yonkers, New York, in 1888, but the first course in North America was in Canada, at the Montreal Golf Club, founded in 1873. However, golf was considered a pretty wussy sport in North America and really didn't catch on in a big way until after World War I. The boost came in 1913, when a former caddy named Francis Ouimet beat two British stars to win the U.S. Open. Since that time, golf has been played in the desert, aboard ships, on the moon, and even below sea level at the Sodom and Gomorrah Golfing Society course on the shore of the Dead Sea.

Alan Shepard used a six-iron (properly called spade mashie) on the moon, in 1971.

Q: It's possible you've never heard the country song "Jambalaya." It's also possible, but less likely, you've never heard "Lovesick Blues" either. The country singer who made both of them smash hits also made "Your Cheatin' Heart," and if you've never heard this song, just turn the page and forget it. Who was the singer?

A: Of course, Hank Williams, or, as he's more often called, the "legendary" Hank Williams.

The Challenge

Q: "Hank" is a diminutive. What is the singer's real name?

A: **Hiram**, although on his birth certificate at Mount Olive, Alabama, it is misspelled (Hiriam).

As for the "legendary" part, there is no dispute. As a performer, he transported audiences into another sphere. According to the late Minnie Pearl, "he just destroyed women in the audience." After the show too, it seems. Although he had married Audrey Mae Sheppard Guy in 1944 – in a gas station – Hank's post-performance escapades led to a divorce in 1952. In October of that year, he married Billy Jean Jones Eshmiller (three times on the same day: two extra times for paying customers at the municipal auditorium in New Orleans). And right in the middle of all this, one of Hank's interim flames, Bobbie Webb Jett, gave birth to their daughter.

Also legendary is Hank's drinking. In his defense, Hank Williams was born with mild spina bifida, a condition aggravated by a horseback-riding injury that doctors treated with megadoses of painkillers. Still, whether to perpetuate his legend, or simply because he was inclined that way, Hank kept on boozing. Shooting guns too. He had a particularly annoying habit of peppering hotel rooms. On one occasion, he fired at a maid, who wisely clobbered him with a table lamp before he could take a second shot. The many failed attempts at clinical treatment are legends of their own. Among the more notable was one at Vanderbilt Hospital, where he checked out before the admission papers could even be set up, and went on a toot that lasted three weeks.

Perhaps as memorable as anything was his death in 1952, in the back seat of a baby-blue Cadillac – where else? – on New Year's Eve. "Your Cheatin' Heart" was released just after this, and became one of the biggest hits that popular music of any kind has ever known.

Q: It's difficult to decide whether this Roman is more famous for crossing the Rubicon or for what Brutus and company did to him. Either way, you know his name. What is it?

A: Indeed, Julius Caesar.

The Challenge

Q: That's not his full name. The first name is missing. What is it?

A: **Gaius.** Julius was his clan name, and Caesar, technically, his surname.

After the Roman Empire collapsed and left a world where people rarely strayed from their birthplace, using only one name — a first name — became commonplace. From the tenth century on, these were almost entirely saints' names. In England, by 1350, fully 64% of the men were Henrys, Johns, Richards, Roberts, and Williams, with William on top. Mary, Elizabeth, and Anne covered 50% of the women.

By the fourteenth century, a more complicated society had resurrected the need for distinctions, the sharpest prod being the need to collect taxes. Thus, William Atbridge (where William lived), who might also be known as William Thomson (especially if Dad was a well-known Tom), or as William Farrier (occupation) or William Red (hair color), was forced to pick one handle and go with it. Naming for saints and biblical figures, however, prevailed right into the late twentieth century, when a flood of one-of-a-kind first names surged in, especially for girls.

Some cultures have rigorously avoided this recent trend. Up to half the boys in some Islamic countries are still called Mohammed. In Korea, about one-sixth of the population is named Kim. These countries also use famous surnames as first names, a practice that came late to the West but is now firmly established. Kennedy is a prime example even though the original Gaelic means "ugly head." In the former U.S.S.R., where religion was suppressed, patriotic parents turned to technology and political science for individuality. Moscow birth records list first names like Electrification and Combine and Hydrostation. They even show a set of twins named Anarchy and Utopia.

85

Q: How do porcupines make love?

A: OK, carefully. The average porky sports over 30,000 quills, but there are none on the underside of the tail. So what happens is that as the male approaches (carefully), the female flattens her tail over her back, and they carry on cautiously. It's definitely not candlelight and wine, but the species sustains itself successfully.

The Challenge

Q: With such a formidable number of barbs, do porcupines ever quill each other?

A: **Yes.** Both sexes are vulnerable on the face and underside. They even quill themselves. If nothing else, this may explain their somewhat torpid mating calisthenics.

No such timidity applies in the case of the Australian red-backed spider. When a male and female catch each other's eye — or antennae, or pheromones — they leap lustily into the fray. (Obviously, there are advantages in being quill-less.) Unfortunately, this plus is more than compensated for in the case of the male, who is eaten by the female right in mid-*flagrante delicto*. She begins at the abdomen and gobbles her way up the body to the male's head, saving to the very last the only remaining item of consequence. The female praying mantis does essentially the same thing, except that she begins with the male's head. (Biologists have established that the brain of the male can halt the release of sperm, so that in quickly removing his head, the female is ensuring that he fulfills his destiny uninterrupted.)

Males of other species who are frightened by such a prospect might prefer to reflect on the copulatory practices of the common housefly as a more appealing alternative. The male of the order Diptera doesn't eat or sleep much after reaching maturity, but spends almost all of its adult life in a conquest to preserve the species. Foreplay, mostly foot-tapping and stroking, is very brief. Actual copulation, however, takes up to an hour. Since the adult male lives only about three weeks, the time-on-task math here reveals a true workaholic, and a level of enthusiasm unmatched by any of the higher-order mammals. Except, perhaps, in triple-X movies.

86

Q: A certain infantry weapon developed during World War II launches a projectile from a simple tube. This device is particularly effective against light tanks. What is it called?

A: Right, a bazooka.

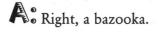

The Challenge

Q: What does a bazooka have in common with a heckelphone, a glass harmonica, and a serpent?

A: They are all musical instruments. The bazooka is a crude mishmash of pipes. It was invented by U.S. comedian Bob Burns in the 1920s, and the military bazooka is actually named after it. Much more peaceful and pleasing is the heckelphone, a double-reed, baritone oboe invented by Wilhelm Heckel at the end of the nineteenth century. Richard Strauss used one in *Salome*. Paul Whitman did too, at his famed Aeolian Hall concert in 1924. The serpent is a snake-shaped bass cornet from the sixteenth century. Mendelssohn, Berlioz, Rossini, and Wagner all used it. Around 1850, it was replaced by the ophicleide, which in turn fell before the bass tuba.

The glass harmonica is a bunch of glasses filled with water to different levels. In 1746, Christoph Gluck played "a concerto on 26 drinking glasses filled with spring water" at the Haymarket Theatre in London. There is no record of what he played, which is not the case for a March 1975 performance on solo violin at Evergreen State College in Washington. Mark Gottlieb played Handel's *Water Music* while immersed in the college swimming pool. Those present felt the acoustical integrity was somewhat compromised because Gottlieb's aggressive bowing stirred up the water. No such analysis is available for the single concert performance so far of David Bedford's "Music For Albion Moonlight" (1956). This piece requires the performer to shout "Hell!" into an open piano to make the strings resonate.

In the face of such advanced creativity in music, it is a relief to learn that other fields, too, boast elevated accomplishment. Sport, for example. In 1975, Kurt Bevacqua of the Milwaukee Brewers won the Bazooka World Series of Bubblegum Blowing by sustaining an eighteen-inch globoid bubble for twelve seconds. He won a year's supply of gum.

87

Q: This sneaky little bacterium hangs out with thousands of buddies in undercooked food, and then, a dozen or so hours after ingestion, really goes to work in the human intestine, often with serious consequences. What's the bacterium called?

A: Yes, salmonella.

The Challenge

Q: It grows in all kinds of food, especially meat, so why *salmon*ella?

A: After veterinarian Daniel E. Salmon (1850–1914).

Although the more than two thousand known varieties of salmonella are sometimes associated with exotic pets like turtles, iguanas, and pygmy hedgehogs, these bugs are mostly found in food. Fortunately for humans, if not for the exotic pets, salmonellae can usually be killed by a good roasting, and a traditional wedding meal of the Bedouin in North Africa provides a remarkable demonstration of this truth. That meal begins with stuffing boiled eggs into roasted fish, which are then stuffed into chickens – also roasted. The chickens, with cargo, are then stuffed into roasted sheep, as many as are necessary to fill a camel. The whole shebang is then roasted for two days and served. Objective (not to mention abstaining) observers claim that salmonella poisoning never occurs after a wedding at which this dish has been featured.

Alcohol, while also known to have some destructive effect on the salmonella bacterium, is not as effective as heat. On the other hand, the case of Viennese troubadour Max Augustin demonstrates the power of alcohol against bubonic plague. In 1697, Augustin, who is celebrated in the song *"Ach du Leiber Augustin,"* was allegedly tossed into a mass grave along with the bodies of several plague victims. After several hours – apparently before the onset of any serious hangover symptoms – he stood up and began singing. And he never did come down with the plague.

The difficulty with alcohol, however, seems to lie in the question of quantification: i.e., just how much protection is needed? The case of George IV of England is illustrative. His death, in 1830, was caused by "rupture of the blood vessels of the stomach, complicated by cirrhosis of the liver, nephritis, dropsy, and gout." But he never had bubonic plague.

174

88

Q: In 1786, American Josiah Shackford made a solo crossing, the first such feat of its kind that we know of. What did he cross?

A: Yes, the Atlantic Ocean. Shackford sailed a fifteen-ton gaff sloop from France to what is now Suriname in thirty-five days.

The Challenge

Q: In 1996–97, Norwegian Boerge Ousland made a solo crossing , also the first of its kind, which took sixty-four days. What did he cross?

A: **Antarctica.** Ousland walked, snowshoed, and skied, towing a sled loaded with 400 pounds (180 kg) of supplies. When the terrain permitted, he strapped on a parachute and let Antarctica's fierce gales tow him. On some days he covered as much as 153 miles (245 km) this way. In comparison, the slow days averaged only about twelve miles (20 km).

When Ousland completed this solo Antarctica crossing, he was already the first on record to ski to both the North and South Poles alone. The first to *see* both poles was Oskar Wisting, the South Pole by surface on December 14, 1911, and the North by flyover on May 12, 1926. (Roald Amundsen always gets the credit but Wisting was right beside him, both trips.) The first to walk to both poles was Robert Swan (South, 1956; North, 1989).

The first surface crossing of Antarctica was led by Sir Vivian Fuchs in 1958 and took ninety-nine days, although he had to pull rank to do it. Fuchs set out from one side with the latest tracked vehicles, heading for the South Pole. From the other side, a party led by Sir Edmund Hillary (yes, the Mount Everest Hillary) was to lay out supplies for Fuchs to use while covering the second half. But Hillary used modified farm tractors, which did better than Fuchs's special snow-travel equipment. Hillary got to the pole first, shot past by 500 miles (800 km), and was going for broke when Sir Vivian made him stop.

No such command structure deterred six British army deserters in 1799. They took off from the garrison at St. Helena on June 10 and rowed to Brazil in thirty-five days. Technically that's still the record for an Atlantic rowing.

89

Q: What is Punxsutawney Phil's claim to fame?

A: Right, he's a Pennsylvania-based groundhog meteorologist that supposedly can predict the end of winter.

The Challenge

Q: What is Pittsburgh Phil's claim to fame?

A: **He was the top hit man for Murder Inc.** Born Harry Strauss in Brooklyn in 1908, he never actually made it to Pittsburgh. Strauss adopted the name Pittsburgh Phil as a way of getting noticed. It must have worked, for crime analysts maintain that by the time Murder Inc. was cracked in 1940 and Pittsburgh Phil was sent to the electric chair at Sing Sing Prison, the provable number of his hits was well in excess of 100. It's no great revelation to learn that among the crime bosses who hired him, Phil was regarded as absolutely dependable.

Although somewhat gruesome, his record is measurably better than the one enjoyed by Punxsutawney Phil, groundhog-in-residence at Punxsutawney, Pennsylvania. Each February 2, this enterprising rodent, with extensive support from the Punxsutawney Chamber of Commerce, is the focus of national attention. Folklore fundamentalists contend that if Phil emerges from his burrow on this day and sees his shadow, only six weeks of winter remain. Unfortunately, over the first sixty years of record keeping, Punxsutawney Phil's hit rate measured out at a paltry 28%. A rival oracle, working out of a burrow in Wiarton, Ontario, under the name "Wiarton Willie," lays claim to a far superior success percentage, but his data have been gathered over a shorter period.

Students of animal behavior might legitimately argue that the weasel (or ermine, in its winter coat) would be a more appropriate pairing for Murder Inc. employees, for it is an uncommonly ferocious predator. Not only that, both species seem to share the same natural enemy. Case in point: In 1937, to make a coronation robe for George VI, the Canadian government sent 50,000 ermine pelts to England. Even Murder Inc. never got into numbers like that.

90

Q: If you are part of a discussion in which the words warp and weft are being used, odds are pretty good that you are talking about what craft?

A: Right, weaving. Warp and weft threads run across each other to make cloth.

The Challenge

Q: Which goes which way?

A. **The lengthwise threads are the warp.** Those crossing from side to side are the weft. Sometimes, the weft is called the woof, but more correctly the woof is the web, which in turn might be a variety of plain weave, commonly called poplin, or a diagonal twill weave often called gabardine, or . . . Well, you see why cloth makers prefer to chat about the weather.

Young Levi Strauss had big warp-and-weft ideas when he arrived in San Francisco during the 1849 gold rush to sell Genoese cotton (called "Genes") for tents. He soon figured out that miners needed pants more than tents, so he shifted to making "waist overalls." In the early 1860s, the young tailor began using a neutral-colored French cloth, *serge de Nîmes* (hence "denim"), a sturdy, more pliant twill. Although it is debated whether he should get the credit for this innovation, Strauss's warp threads were dyed indigo blue, thus minimizing the visibility of dirt.

His next modification, in 1873, addressed complaints about splitting pocket seams. In the camps, Strauss watched miners squatting to pan for gold and noted the points of stress. Thus came rivets, not just on the pockets but on the crotch. The latter addition was a near disaster for Strauss, for when exposed to direct sunlight during panning, or a campfire during cooking, this crucially placed stud caused painful hot spots. It was quickly dropped, but pocket rivets hung on until the 1930s when school principals raised a hue about scratched desks.

Unlike the reputation of Levi Strauss, that of his contemporary Amelia Bloomer unjustifiably ignores her place in the history of warp and weft. Her objection to hoop skirts was not just a case of feminist principles in action. At the time, crinolines were woven of stiff linen and horsehair. And you think rivets were a problem.

91

Q: On your way to outer space, you must first travel through the bottom layer of air around Earth. It's called the troposphere. That's the first 10 miles (15 kilometers) or so. The next layer goes up to about 30 miles (50 km). What is this layer called?

A: Correct, the stratosphere. Then comes the mesosphere, to 50 miles (80 km), the thermosphere above that, and finally, if your booster is really hot, you hit the exosphere.

The Challenge

Q: When do you hit "outer space"?

A. **At 50 miles (80 km), when you clear the mesosphere.**

In 1942, the German rocket program was first to get up there, with an A4 rocket (the name was later changed to V-2) which topped out at 52 miles (84 km). That was from their test site in Peenemunde. Two years later, the same team got way into outer space when they launched an A4 from Poland to just over double the height of their first shot. Only twenty-eight years after that, on March 2, 1972, the United States launched *Pioneer 10*, the first craft to leave the solar system. When the craft crossed Pluto's orbit in October 1986, *Pioneer 10* was 3,666,000,000 miles (just under six billion km) from Earth.

For those of us boggled by the pace of technological development, these data become even more intimidating by comparing them to the results of the first recorded attempt at a rocket launch. That was in April 1750, almost two hundred years before the first A4 launch. A group of British artillerymen got their missile – all of three inches (7.62 cm) in diameter – to shoot up 3,748 feet (1,142 m). (Or so they reported. There was ample verification that the rocket went up, way up. But it's not clear how such a precise height was determined.)

In light of these achievements, it's almost hard to be amazed that in 1991 a Florida mailman, Dennis La Mothe, working out of his garage, built a 35-foot (10.6-m) rocket called *Downright Ignorant* which achieved an altitude of 3,440 feet (1,048 m). More charming, perhaps, is that the nose cone of *Downright Ignorant* was the genuine article (military surplus). Mrs. La Mothe had bought it at a garage sale, where it was being offered for one dollar and touted as a one-of-a-kind flowerpot.

Q: When journalist/playwright L. Frank Baum published *Mother Goose in Prose* in 1897, he had a real hit on his hands. Then, in 1900, he had an even bigger smash with a book about a Kansas farm girl caught in a tornado and stranded in Munchkin Land. The movie based on this book has been in continual release since 1939, and of course you know the movie's title. It is . . . ?

A: Indeed, *The Wizard of Oz.*

The Challenge

Q: What is the title of the book?

A: *The Wonderful Wizard of Oz.* Baum's title is almost never cited accurately. Most of the time, the "wonderful" is dropped, as it was for the movie and for the 1901 smash-hit musical. Names get short shrift in the movie too. Dorothy's last name is Gayle, but see how often you catch that in the movie. Or the wizard's full name; it's Oscar Zoraster Phadrig Isaac Norman Henkle Emmanuel Ambroise Diggs.

Like all cultural icons, this movie has some wonderful tales about it. For example, MGM wanted Jerome Kern to write the music but he was ill, so they turned to Harold Arlen and "Yip" Harburg. "Over the Rainbow" was cut by Louis B. Mayer and then restored. It won the Oscar for Best Song, but the movie itself lost to *Gone with the Wind.* For the part of Dorothy, MGM originally wanted Shirley Temple so badly that they offered both Clark Gable and Jean Harlow to Fox in a trade, but Harlow's unfortunate death put an end to the negotiations. Actor Frank Morgan did yeoman service in the movie, playing five roles: the wizard, Professor Marvel, guards in the Emerald City and the wizard's chamber, and coachman.

By modern standards *The Wizard of Oz* was a cheapie, with or without the "wonderful," for it came in under $3 million. To put that figure in perspective, however, another big hit, *The Great Train Robbery*, shot in New Jersey in 1903, cost $150. The real winner on a cost-per-minute basis is the first motion picture ever to be submitted for copyright in the U.S. It was shot in 1894, in black and white, and shows a man in the act of sneezing. Total cost: $7.50.

93

Q: Lobsters are found in all the world's oceans, but lobsters with large front claws are found only in one. Where are these clawed lobsters found?

A: Right, the Atlantic Ocean; specifically, the North Atlantic. The claws, incidentally, are a radically developed pair of front legs. Both the male and female have them.

The Challenge

Q: How can you distinguish male from female lobsters by sight?

A: With difficulty. (You may have to pick them up.) Female lobsters have pincers (for grooming their eggs) on the fifth set of legs. They also have feathery appendages on the abdomen, also for taking care of their eggs. Neither feature is easy to spot. This could explain why lobsters' eyes — the males' anyway — are raised and can rotate full circle.

Eyeballs seem to have an interesting and mobile time in the ocean. One of the most dramatic examples is on the halibut, which begins life with an eye on either side of its head, but as it matures, the body flattens, and one eye slowly migrates to join the other. The California sheephead, on the other hand, lives its life in an entirely mundane fashion, ophthalmically speaking, but compensates by beginning life as a female and gradually becoming a male. Another type that changes sex is the angelfish.

Fish may one day turn out to be the final arbiter in the great debate over whether it's truly possible to be both sexy and smart. For example, the body of a three-foot female Atlantic cod (in this fish, guys are guys and girls are girls, and they stay that way) outweighs its brain by a factor of 5,000. Yet this same cod may produce up to five million eggs. Ichthyologists acknowledge that they have not yet worked out what the body-brain relationship has to do with productive power, but it is tempting to draw conclusions.

The cod is the unofficial provincial fish of Newfoundland. The garibaldi is the official state fish of California. Bolivia does not have a state fish. Nor does Malawi. Wisconsin doesn't either, but it has a state dance. The polka was made official in 1994.

94

Q: This impressive engineering and construction achievement, completed in 1935, straddles the Colorado River in the U.S.A. One end is anchored in Arizona and the other in Nevada. It's the . . . ?

A: Sure, the Hoover Dam.

The Challenge

Q: Who is it named for?

A: Secretary of Commerce Hoover (not President Hoover) in the Coolidge administration.

Life is full of disappointments like this. The Hundred Years War, for example, was really The Hundred and Sixteen Years War (between England and France, from 1337 to 1453). Chinese Checkers was invented in Sweden. The Douglas fir is actually a pine. Tennessee Williams was born in Missouri. Venetian blinds were invented by the Japanese. The Battle of Bunker Hill was fought at Breed's Hill. The Canary Islands are named after wild dogs, not birds. And Aaron Copland's *Appalachian Spring* premiered in the fall.

Given all the above, it should be no surprise that the famous Woodstock Festival of 1969 was actually at Bethel, NY, and that the Battle of Waterloo was fought somewhat south of Waterloo, between Mont-Saint-Jean and Belle-Alliance. Even a campaign slogan that President Hoover would have probably preferred to forget, "a chicken in every pot," was in fact recycled from France's Henry IV. Around 1600 – during a recession – Henry proclaimed his plan to make the country so prosperous that "every peasant will have a chicken in his pot on Sunday." Some comfort, however, can be derived from knowing that Ulysses S. Grant is actually buried in Grant's Tomb, although strictly speaking his body is entombed there, not buried.

The Hoover Dam is a significant piece of work – concrete was poured continually for two years – but in terms of size, it is pretty much dwarfed by ranges of dams in Canada, Argentina, and Russia. Thus, it could be that when docents at the Hoover complex call it a "miracle," they are referring to the fact that it needed the close and continued cooperation of six states and the federal government, and was still completed in only seven years.

95

Q: Comedian Jimmy Durante used to end his radio and TV shows with a special "Good night" to someone. He would always say "Good night" to Mrs. . . . . Mrs. whom?

A: Yes, Mrs. Calabash. What he said was, "Good night, Mrs. Calabash, wherever you are."

The Challenge

Q: Where was she?

A. **In Calabash, North Carolina.** She was a restaurant owner named Lucy Coleman. Durante and his touring entourage stopped by for a meal one day, and the comedian, apparently impressed with Mrs. Coleman and restaurant, promised to make her famous. And he did. "Good night, Mrs. Calabash" remained a trademark of Durante's for almost forty years until his death in 1980. Mrs. Coleman, despite the attention the phrase attracted, steadfastly declined any interviews and assiduously avoided the media spotlight until her own death in 1989. She did once admit, however, that on that day in her restaurant, she had no idea who Durante was.

Jimmy Durante insured his nose with Lloyd's of London for $140,000. Betty Grable's legs were insured for $250,000, while Fred Astaire's were covered for $650,000. Lloyd's also carried a policy on Jose Greco's pants for $980. They were custom sewn so they wouldn't split on stage, but no seams are perfect, apparently. None of these policies was ever paid out. Nor did Lloyd's ever have to cough up on a rash of agreements it sold in the late 1950s, insuring against a "falling Sputnik" (annual premium $74). Because it does not sell life insurance, Lloyd's was not involved in the claim by George Armstrong Custer's beneficiaries after the battle of the Little Big Horn. The policy was for $5,000; interesting planning on Custer's part. We can't be sure, but it may have been spurred by some of his experiences in the West, one of the more notable being in 1867, when he shot his own horse in the back of the head during a buffalo hunt.

Insurance companies rank the following professionals as their top risks: astronauts, test pilots, stunt people, toreadors, hot-air balloonists, large-animal trainers, and trapeze artists who perform without nets.

Q: During World War II, German scientists at Peenemunde, Germany, found that *Vergeltungswaffe-eins* and *Vergeltungswaffe-zwei* took too long to say, let alone write, so they used abbreviations for these missiles. What abbreviations?

A: Yes, V-1 and V-2. These unstoppable but wildly inaccurate rockets were called "buzz bombs" in England. In German, the term means "revenge (or reprisal) weapon."

The Challenge

Q: In standard dictionaries, are the V-1 and V-2 entries at the beginning or the end of the Vs?

A̶° Near the end. Numbers, in these cases, are treated as words, so that "V-One" comes after a word like voltmeter but before a word like voodoo.

Neither V-1 nor V-2 appeared in British dictionaries of the 1940s, possibly because lexicographers believed Lord Cherwell, scientific advisor to Churchill, who assured the government that German rocket-propelled bombs were nothing but a propaganda rumor. Between the summer of 1944 and the spring of 1945, just under 7,000 of these rumors were launched at Britain. Despite Cherwell's significant accomplishments in math and physics, he is regrettably well known for this goof. And he's not alone. William Thomson (First Baron Kelvin, 1824–1907), a major contributor to science (with items like a tide predictor, harmonic analyzer, and more), went zero for three with the following while he was president of the Royal Society: "Radio has no future"; "Heavier than air flying machines are impossible"; and "X-rays will prove to be a hoax." Then there's the gem by a Cambridge University professor of aeronautical engineering when he saw Frank Whittle's design for a jet engine in 1941: "Very interesting, Whittle, my boy, but it'll never work."

Not that any one nation has a corner on tunnel vision. In 1945, the United States brought over Werner von Braun and other German scientists from Peenemunde. One of their first requests was for any papers by U.S. scientist and inventor Robert Goddard that might not have been available to them in Europe. Goddard had launched the world's first liquid-fueled rocket at Roswell, New Mexico, in 1926, and the Germans had used his findings extensively. Von Braun was shocked to discover that most scientists on Goddard's home turf knew almost nothing about his work.

97

Q: Unlike his 1875 opera, *Carmen*, which gets international play on a regular basis, Bizet's opera of some thirteen years before is hardly ever performed. Yet a duet taken from this opera about fishermen gets performed all the time. What do the singers of this duet fish for in the opera?

A: Right, pearls. The song is from *The Pearl Fishers*, or, as Bizet wrote it, *Les Pêcheurs de perles*. In the duet, two pearl fishermen make up after having become estranged during a love affair with the same woman.

The Challenge

Q: In what country are these pearl fishers doing their diving (and singing)?

A: Ceylon (modern-day Sri Lanka).

The limited performance of this work should not be attributed to Bizet's choice of Ceylon. After all, he could hardly be expected to have his characters compete with Wagner for space in the Rhine. Besides, who knows just why some works make it and others don't?

Some operas have achieved obscurity despite the promise in their titles: e.g., Condell's *Love Laughs at Locksmiths* (1803) and Arnold's *Genius of Nonsense, an Original, Whimsical, Operatical, Pantomimical, Farcical, Electrical, Naval, and Military Extravaganza* (1784).

A more modern opus lingering in darkness is *The Life and Times of Josef Stalin* by American Robert Wilson. Not only does the title sound like an educational-film snooze, performing it takes thirteen and a half hours. No wonder the work surged to the bottom of the repertoire on opening night in December 1973. Yet another opera you're not likely to hear soon (mercifully) is Paul Hindemith's 1929 *Nues vom Tage*, in part because of an injunction taken out by the Breslau Gas Company. In one scene, the heroine takes a bath in water heated electrically and sings "constant hot water, no horrid smell, no danger of explosion."

Depending on the materials used, there is sometimes a smell at the end of Mozart's *Don Giovanni* when the Don descends into hell, usually through a trap door and usually in a great swirl of smoke. At a memorable performance in Dublin, the descent mechanism failed, and when the smoke cleared, Don Giovanni was still on Earth – from the waist up. People in the audience sat in shocked, silent unease until a wag in the balcony broke them up by shouting, "Thank God! Hell's full at last!"

98

Q: When European sportscasters report on football's Super Bowl (most ignore it), they call the game American football. What do North Americans call "football" as it is played in Europe?

A: Yes, soccer.

The Challenge

Q: What should they call it?

A. **Association football.** Over 140 countries play "football" by rules drawn up in a British pub in 1863. (The U.S. is the only country in the world that plays American football.)

The game is subject to the most confusing differences internationally. Several countries that belong to FIFA (*Fédération Internationale de Football Association*), the governing body of football formed in 1904, also play rugby football, and Gaelic football and Australian rules football, all different. Canada plays Canadian football, a mix of rugby and American football.

It's possible that football was simply predestined to be mixed up. Take McGill University's invitation from Harvard for an exhibition game in the fall of 1874. As soon as the ball was snapped, the two teams discovered they were operating by different sets of rules. Under an *ad hoc* compromise, they tried both sets, and found that each had good ideas for the other, but there was no final meeting of minds. Canadian football, over a century later, still has a larger field, twelve-man teams, only three downs, and more action.

One element that all football variations seem to share, even though there are penalties for it, is rough play. (The penalty is usually called "unnecessary rough play"; note that this is not the rule invoked when a referee is shot, as has happened in Latin America.) There seems to be ample historical tradition for the violence too. In the British Isles, the idea of having dedicated playing fields developed principally to protect town sites from players and spectators. President Teddy Roosevelt, no powder puff himself, threatened to abolish the American game entirely in 1906. A French writer in 1754, after seeing a game in England, commented that "if this is playing, it is impossible to tell what they might call fighting."

99

Q: What U.S. island hosted the planet's longest recorded volcanic eruption?

A: Right, Hawaii. Kilauea started pouring out lava in 1983, and ten years later was still pumping past the known record.

The Challenge

Q: What Indonesian island hosted the planet's loudest recorded volcanic eruption?

A. **Krakatoa,** in one massive blow on August 27, 1883, at 3 a.m. GMT. The sound was heard over one-thirteenth of the earth's surface. Using a range of data set down at the time, vulcanologists calculate that this explosion must have had at least twenty-six times the power of the biggest-ever H-bomb test. Since the shock wave from that one (in the U.S.S.R. on October 30, 1961) circled the globe three times, at a factor of twenty-six it's not hard to understand why parts of the island of Krakatoa came down in Australia two weeks after the eruption.

Solid matter and gas both expand in the upper atmosphere, a bit of science that may have importance for those who tend to be flatulent. The typical human colon holds about six cubic inches (100 cubic centimeters) of gas, but this can expand as much as sevenfold at the altitudes normally reached by passenger jets, which therefore makes eating an onion-and-bean casserole just before takeoff a very bad idea. Even more interesting is the Krakatoa-like potency of this chiefly methane/hydrogen mixture, as reported by Minneapolis physician J. H. Bond in *Gastrointestinal Endoscopy* (1976). While cauterizing polyps in the colon of a seventy-one-year-old male, the good doctor was blown across the room, along with accompanying jets of blue flame. Both doctor and patient recovered, although the latter needed surgical repairs.

No such recourse was available to Hilton Martin of Florida, whose toilet blew up (1985) after he cleaned the bowl with Comet and hung a Sani-Flush dispenser inside. The concatenation, investigators concluded, was the result of combining sodium hypochlorite and sodium bisulfate in a confined space. So much for putting the lid down.

100

Q: At the Metropolitan Museum in New York, a wall menu that once hung in a drinking emporium in ancient Babylon offers dark beer, pale beer, red beer, beer with or without a head, and more; not unlike pubs today. But all these beers, despite several thousand years of brewing, still come in two basic types. What are they?

A: Right, ale and lager.

The Challenge

Q: What's the difference?

A. The rise or fall of the yeast. Ale is top-fermented; the yeast rises. Lager, on the other hand, is bottom-fermented; the yeast settles.

For centuries, all yeasts rose during fermentation. No one understood why, but since English brewers for one called the stuff *godisgood*, they obviously weren't about to look a gift horse in the mouth. The first mention of lager is from Bavaria in the 1400s. Brewers began to store, or "lager," their brew in alpine caves, where in the cool environment the yeast settled, leaving a different taste and, most of the time, a clearer liquid. Not until artificial refrigeration in the mid-nineteenth century, however, did lager brewing become universal. Australians and Americans led the way, a fact which may explain the strong preference in those countries for bland lagers served ice-cold. Other major brewing countries – Germany, Britain, Canada, Belgium, and Korea, for example – tend to offer more ales as well as tastier lagers, both of which can, and should, be served warmer.

Beer is one of humanity's great links. Caesar toasted his officers with beer after crossing the Rubicon. Elizabeth I, when she traveled, sent couriers ahead to test whether local beers were up to snuff. Finland's national epic, the *Kavela*, devotes 200 verses to the creation of the world but 400 to the origin of beer. The Babylonians fussed over issues like whether bar patrons should be permitted to drink standing up. (Standing drinkers, their publicans claimed, get into fights.)

Until 1968, it was illegal to drink beer standing up in Manitoba. Presumably, by that time, Manitobans had learned to control themselves. However, it continues to be illegal there to drink beer in a privy. Obviously there are limits to just how much self-control can be expected in that province.